21.

Sheila E. Harvey.

See Page 147.

Sheila E. Harvey.

ARRIVAL PRESS

THE CIRCLE OF LIFE

Edited

By

TIM SHARP

First published in Great Britain in 1996 by
ARRIVAL PRESS
1 - 2 Wainman Road, Woodston,
Peterborough, PE2 7BU

HB ISBN 1 85786 412 3
SB ISBN 1 85786 407 7

Foreword

From the moment of conception, the circle of life begins. This includes; birth, growing up, adolescence, marriage, right through to our eventual demise.

The poetry contained in this anthology reflects our journey through life.

Whilst editing this book it became apparent that life has so many periods of joy, sadness and trauma. I think after reading this book you will agree with me that the *Circle of Life* is a true reflection of these periods.

Tim Sharp
Editor

CONTENTS

THE CLOSING OF THE CIRCLE

And as she heard the time tick by
while she sang her baby a lullaby,
faded on her face was the careless look
as the great responsibility she took.

And as she sang a happy song
with all her children singing along,
she saw her ring fitting tight
on the hand that once was slim and light.

And as she talked of life to her teens
and built with them beautiful dreams,
her curly head in a bright sun ray
showed hundreds of strands of shiny grey.

And as she kissed her kids good-bye
for alone at last they had to fly,
she was sad, and yet was strong,
for half her life was now gone.

And as she reached for love one morning
her life companion was quickly warning
that his love for her was over and done,
and in a few days he would be gone.

And as she looked at cloudy skies
waiting for calls and letters to arrive,
a childhood friend she thought she'd lost
settled in her home like morning frost.

And as she sipped her morning tea
her childhood dreams now lost at sea,
her loyal friend she embraced with gratitude
with a cold chill she welcomed solitude.

Alex A-Nicotera

THE WET WINDOW PANE

His faded blue eyes gazed around at his farm
As he shielded his face with his hand
And he flinched at the sounds that invaded his world
He was watching the death of his land

He looked at the soil that was cracking from thirst
At the crop that had withered and died
Then he was aware of a hand on his arm
As his wife silently stood by his side

She knew with the wisdom of women since Eve
That they could not exist without rain
She ached with a longing that women endure
When they witness their husband in pain

He sighed as he turned and gazed at her face
His hand gently touching her hand
The wind whipped away quiet words that he spoke
As they turned with their backs to the land

The terrible wind that had killed off the crops
Corroding and cracking the soil
Still screamed all around . . . like a woman in pain
And mocked at their back-breaking toil

They quietly sat in the house he had built
Where she had arrived as a bride
With the furniture polished and treated with care
Each item he'd made with such pride

She cooked him a meal that was fit for a king
While the wind screamed in fury outside
Then they lay down together to spend their last night
She slept as the old farmer cried

2

They were found by a stranger the very next day
As he gazed through their wet window pane
Their souls had departed, along with the wind
Unaware it had started to rain.

Moby

THE CIRCLE OF LIFE

Those childhood days all spent on farm,
So free to roam, no fear of harm;
The cattle, horses, pigs and sheep,
Provided lessons for life to keep.

The village school so full of life,
With work and play and little strife;
Some poems, tables, learnt by heart,
The basics there for a sound start.

The Army called in time of need,
For folk to serve and do great deeds;
The training, fitness were so great,
The NCO's they were first rate.

A life with students young and old,
Their souls and hearts one helped to mould;
You see them act and work and shine,
They make one proud to meet and dine.

As sunset falls upon one's life,
And more time spent with loving wife,
The pictures, memories from first to last,
All serve reminders of times long past.

John Paulley

3

YOU'LL BE A MAN MY SON

Fourteen is a funny age, but bear it if you can,
No longer are you a little boy, nor yet are you a man,
It's an age of contradictions and much frustration too,
You may get cross that everyone expects so much of you,
You'll feel that you are now too old by rules to be enclosed,
It may be hard to understand the disciplines imposed.
Yet there will be times you'll feel too young for the wisdom we expect,
But, you must learn to think things out, independently reflect.
Learn to stand on your own feet, make decisions when you can,
From now on you're in training for when you become a man.

For development of character be logical and fair,
Keep your temper in control, of your own faults be aware,
At school you must remember there is much work to be done,
We know what your potential is, so it's up to you my son.
There are sixty golden minutes in every golden hour,
To waste each one is foolish, but used wisely to devour -
A book, a word or a tiny piece of meaningful, useful knowledge,
Is the kind of wisdom you will need, if you wish to get to college.
It may sound hard, but it's not all work, there will still be time for play,
Just choose your pastimes carefully, do not fritter time away.

Ruby Lawrence

THE THIRD AGE

They say that we're past it and haven't a clue,
we're old fashioned and set in our ways.
But our minds are now clearer and free of all stress.
We have come to our own golden days.

In our book of life many pages we wrote.
From encounters with life we have learned.
Many knocks in the past, our character formed,
and all evil and bad thoughts we spurned.

4

Now we have the leisure to do as we will.
Our hobbies and sports we pursue.
We've plenty of time to travel at will.
whatever we like we can do.

So don't be afraid if you're getting old,
it's really a marvellous age.
The best is to come, in the great book of life
we're writing another new page.

Fred Wyer

THE END OF THE FAMILY LINE

I see my mother
Reflected in the glass
When I wear her old dress.

I write my father
On every cheque
The symphony of 'Burton'.

I hear my grandmother
In words and phrases
That I utter.

I feel my Grandfather
At football matches.
Cheering, next to me.
But, it can never be.

I am all of them . . .
And, yet,
Myself alone.

Nick Brunel

CONGRUOUS SORROW

As twilight snows
upon you in life,
when times seem choked
with stress and strife

Let life not trouble you,
try as it may,
be strong, be brave,
wipe your tears away

Lay down your anxiety
it causes you pain,
if you do
you will surely gain

When loved ones depart
please try not to grieve,
For your pain keeps them
here and they cannot leave

Let peace become them,
they are happy you see,
You would be too,
if you were free

Just pick up the pieces
and carry on,
for the day will come
when you too will be gone

Peter Charles Gooding

TWILIGHT

No, I'm not old, not really,
Just 'Of the older generation'.
It's the turn of my sons to breathe, 'O Mother',
And sigh in exasperation.
Once I thought, old age would come unnoticed,
Gradually the years would release
Wisdom and deep serenity,
Calm acceptance and quiet peace.

In any 'home' you will find them,
Knees swathed in blanket and shawl,
Asleep, heads back, mouths fallen open,
Or staring, unseeing, at the wall.
Dulled are the intellects once so keen,
Limbs once active shuffle and stumble;
Eyes that were bright now faded dim.
Lips once articulate mutter and mumble.
Occasionally a chair will be empty
'Not well-lately she's not been the same',
A look of fear or resignation -
They know it's a waiting game.

But I'm not old, not yet.
There it is, I've had my say,
Must get up, keep busy -
There are lots of jobs to do today.
Hens need cleaning, straw needs turning,
Leaves to sweep and set to burning,
Clean the car, fix the tap,
But before I do -
Just a little nap?

Marie Roberts

REFLECTIONS

If I could be as a child again; and see as a child could see;
A different world would unfold itself; innocent, wide-eyed and free.
I'd view the scene like a fairy-tale, where nothing could go wrong.
Where the outstretched hands would be safe, and true; the ideals of
                                                    men be strong.

In the concrete jungle, lost I'd be; I'd long for the open fields,
Where children played, and the world seemed safe; a childhood secret yields.
The innocence of youthful minds, if only it could last,
But life goes on, and we grow up - our infant days are past.

So, through our teens; then marriage vows; our family soon complete.
For then we've children of our own - our home life now replete.
Full circle in our lives has come, nostalgic thoughts are frequent,
Turn back the clock; remember youth - those times forever poignant.

We see ourselves as we were then, in days so long ago,
Our footprints were as yet untrod, on newly fallen snow.
Yet, through our lives, each step we take, will surely be recorded,
We'll answer for the things we've done; the good will be applauded.

We may wish to protect from the stress of life, but we all had to learn,
It's part of testing life itself; no need for wealth, to yearn.
Just be content with what you have; watch a child on someone's knee -
Reflections of our childhood days in their bright eyes we'll see.

Jan Portlock-Barker

LAURA

The miracle of birth
Surprises and delights.
The helplessness of this tiny being
Takes the breath away.
She brings such joy.

Soon there will be other emotions:
Panic,
Sleepless nights,
Coping alone.
But the joy will sustain.

Mary Bailey

ROUND HOLE IN A SQUARE PEG

Hello girl, hello boy, who are you inside?
Are you going to let us see the turning of the tide?
Bring out your true identity,
Show us who you are.
We're going to miss you when you're gone,
When you're travelling afar.

You've been fair and you've been dark,
You've been all the different shades
But you're facing now the biggest change,
as your false appearance fades.
What will emerge from the surgeon's intervention?
And what will become of the hormone prevention?

I hope you get your dream,
and your gender transformations.
Successfully shed your past,
and overcome the limitations.
Wear your lips and lashes and skirts for real.
Hold your head up high like a pillar of steel.

You've been the hostess with the mostest,
Been the life and soul of the parties, been the boldest.
Country girl and small town boy,
Wait 'till you get your new toy.

Darren Martin Austin

THE DANCE OF LIFE

In youth the dance calls to us, and we rush to join the fun,
into life's waiting ballroom, for the music has just begun.
With lilting strains it beckons us as into the swaying throng,
with heads held high in elation we re-echo the haunting song.

And in the whirling frenzy, as the dancers go hurtling past,
each maid must seek a partner; each lad must find a lass.
Each pair must match the tempo - no matter how mad the pace,
for in youth our feet tread swiftly, we see nought but each other's face.

But the dancers now are tiring, some partners have left the room,
and the ballroom clock strikes midnight with loud and sonorous boom.
Yet we cling to each other more closely, as the Last Waltz begins to play,
and your whispered words are more dear to me,
as we dance at the end of the day.

Dorothy Brookes

TREE SEASONS

I wonder at the flowers attended by the bees,
I marvel at white horses riding high upon the sea
But if I had to choose what really pleases me
It's the beauty and the grandeur and variety of trees.

They humbly come from seeds but in stature quickly grow,
Many times when huge in girth and height a century or more.
They shade us from the glaring sun, give shelter from the snow
And protect next season's flowers by leaves scattered on the floor.

I so enjoy the leaves all bright and green in spring.
Or, in the heat, the heavier summer bower birds do sing
Don't forget the russets and the golds that autumn brings
And their stark nakedness in winter, birds gone upon the wing.

Eileen Jolly

GAYLE

The day no longer
  Hides the sadness
So I will sleep
  The whole day through,
My eyes will open
  To the darkness
And in the darkness
  Will be you . . .

Gerald Aldred Judge

THE WEAVING

The evening moon, low in the sky, and bright,
Hangs like a Persian lamp behind the tree,
Clouds that are knotted edges of a mat
Placed on the sand, cover the gentle light.
Now there begins the weaving of a robe;
Older than time, made where the leaves linger;
Where they too, add patterns. Where the great one;
The master of the weaving envelopes
The loom with the light of his silver sleeve.
Half hidden behind a chequered door;
Working with shadows, his eyes drawn far away.
There, glow stars and horses, and shells scattered
Among the bright plumes of an ocean floor.
Softly, while others sleep in the dark room,
Behold, a garment wider than the night!
Then the weaver, brushing aside his tears,
Adds a signature: All of unending life's
Perplexing multitude of tyrannies,
Broider the gown, moon bright, that the world wears.

Margaret Dove

WHAT A LIFE

Your start in life is a big mishap
As soon as you arrive you get a slap
From then on you never do anything right
You're sleeping all day and crying all night

You're sent off to school when you want to stay home
And you have to stay in when you want to roam
Then you go out to work and you get cash in hand
But it runs through your fingers like the hour glass sand

Now you're trying to keep the loan sharks at bay
There's the mortgage, electric and gas bills to pay
Then you retire at last, what a larf
That's not the end of your troubles not half

Then you pop your clogs, arrive at the golden gate
There stand St Peter says half a mo mate
The boss wants to see you, and indeed he did
He told me I owed him 15 quid

Well I couldn't pay him there was no way
So he sent me back for another stay
So her I am, unseen I agree
When something goes missing you can bet it's me

Gilbert H Waudy

WHAT WILL BE WILL BE!

Born in the sunshine
Christened in the rain
Married in the winter time
Divorced feeling pain

Met a new love in the spring time
Fell in love and saw the sun
Even in the years of autumn
The Circle of Life goes on!

Irene Dyce

PAST PRESENT FUTURE

I lie awake
I dream
A thought
Of era's past
Of future sought
The present

For what we see
For what we hear
For what we smell
For what we feel
For what we taste
For what we sense
Are but seconds in the past

A fleeting thought
A sight
A sound
A quiet footstep on the ground
A nod of head
A weary blink
A postcard which will make you think
The thoughts of yesteryear

No future here
For time is strife
Fountains made
The rock of life

Keith Hall

WHAT IS LOVE?

What is love?

Is it hearts and flowers
Kisses one, two, three
Then a romantic dinner
Proposal on one knee?

> Is it just an emotion
> When you stand and say 'I do'
> Arrayed in all your finery
> All eyes upon you two?

No
It's standing shoulder to shoulder
When you haven't made the grade
When you know that you're a failure
You're lonely and afraid.
> It's walking at midnight
> When your partner's got a 'bad head'
> Talking the problem over
> Then cuddling up in bed.
It's getting up in the morning
After the quarrel late last night
Saying that you're sorry
And calling off the fight.

It's being there for someone
When everything's gone wrong.
It's laughing, encouraging, listening
Commitment all life long.

G M Thomas

FROM NOWHERE TO ETERNITY

Somewhere in the distant past lies nowhere,
The land in which there was no 'US'
Before we met, alone - we used to live there
Till one day it became the land that was.

To new and greener pastures we conspired,
My hand in yours, so, gently, we moved on.
We learned of love, so very much admired;
For us the land of nowhere soon was gone.

Day after day the joy of love grew greater.
With children we sealed our union soon.-
As I am putting words upon this paper,
Each memory a star, a glowing moon. -

The years went by, we lived through them together,
Transformed were 'You' and 'I' into one 'US'
So strong, so gentle, through all stormy weather
We knew, our love would open up a pass.

Then one day came, it really was a noneday,
On which a door was opened just for you;
And you stepped through - for me this was Black Monday -
Alone again? Once more a separate 'Two?'

No wall, no door, no time, no space is separation,
For our love is deep and good and strong.
This life on earth we live in preparation
To spend eternity singing love's wondrous song.

A song of love, a song for us, oh hold me close my Darling,
I love you so, you are my life, just hold me tight
Until I see you one fine glorious morning -
Eternally 'US' - till then, my love, Good Night.

Helga Dharmpaul

THE BUMP

Its a strange and wonderful feeling
Whilst laying in your bed
When your partner leans
across you
and listens with his head
To the child that
grows inside you
To the heart that beats away
Two people looking forward
to a very special day

Allyson Burrows

I HAVE A DREAM

I have a dream
Like many in the past
of the *All Perfect World*
Will it come
will it last

Yes I have a dream
of years from now
When the world will change
Some-day some-how

I have a dream
That some fine day
We'll see Lions and Lambs
Involved in play

I have a dream
Just wait and see
That one day there won't be
not a single *Enemy*!

D A Walker

FULL CIRCLE

So tiny helpless
The day you were born,
I feel such love for you
You look so forlorn.

For years you depend on me
I feel so strong
You look up to me
I can do no wrong.

The rows start to come
And we drift apart.
We have nothing in common
And it breaks my heart.

I've long since retired
My health starts to go
How long have I got?
I just don't know.

You come to see me
How old you have grown
Your face looks like one
I used to own.

You look at me
In my hospital bed
'I'll take care of you'
Was all you said

So life turns a circle
From father to son,
From son to father
We all become one.

Mary Wood

FREE SPIRIT

Fly away free spirit
Soar high into the sky
To watch the circle turn
The cycle begin again

The seeds of spring are planted
The youth of life steps forth
Seedlings steadily growing
Nourished, nurtured and adored

In the warmth of summer's glow
So in harmony and tune
Young fruit ripening, maturing
Blossoming - flowers in full bloom

As autumn mists descend
Nature mellows with age
The fragile circle turns again
Colours wane and fade

Gripped in the cold of winter
When the earth lies barren and bare
Begins the time for renewal
Memories and experiences to share

Now the cycle has turned full circle
The journey through life has ceased
So fly away free spirit
To find rest in eternal peace.

Patricia O'Gorman

SHIPWRECKED ON THE EVENING TIDE

Here I lie shipwrecked and weary;
Senseless on the shore.
Yet, now I see quite clearly
A truth that I'd never seen before.

Once I sailed in mid-channel, free,
Sails unfurled to the sun.
Confident winds blustered 'round me -
Buoyant with her heart they'd won.

With this storm, hope has drowned,
But - at least - I've tried!
All thoughts and dreams have run aground -
Waiting for the evening tide.

Rotting hulks are littered 'round me -
Love and hate and lust and fear.
The clawing surf was where fate found me,
Like all the wrecks that are beached here.

Now, with frantic hand,
Marooned amid the silence of the beach,
Scratching messages in the sand
To a soul that I cannot reach.

The sun became a bleeding heart adrift on a silver foil sea,
As desolate as fluttering rags on decaying timbers
(The sailcloth that once drove me)'
Until the ocean extinguished its dying embers.

Perhaps I should abandon my odyssey
With the remnants of my shattered pride,
Succumb to this thing that spurned me,
And leave the other wanderers to the tide.

Nicola Barnes

LEAP YEAR DAY

February the twenty ninth; re-appears, once in every four years,
Ladies, down on one knee, can propose matrimony.

My darling I offer you my life,
Will you make me your wife.

Keeping you only by my side

For better you and I,
Together we will grow, to overcome, for worst.

Through life our love, for richer in abundance will overflow
Guiding us through for poorer, how important
The necessities of life, money cannot buy.

In sickness a passage through our lives
Like a bubble it could burst.

Strength we will find.
Strength within our marriage, in health, body, and mind.

To love affectionately, to cherish as one
Always to care, be each other's guide.

Till death, only then and when we have no other choice
In love, in spirit, on the other side.

Lizzie

WHAT IS LIFE?

When you've read all the words
That there are, to be read
And you've seen all there is
To be seen,
When you've heard all the sounds
Made by Nature and Man, and
Felt all the pain, there has been.

When a world full of joy has
Been felt in your heart, with the
Total of man's hate for man,
It is then, only then, you may
Hazard a guess, at what
Life is; if anyone can!

G C Garbutt

TO MUM

Many years have passed since you first held me in your palms,
And my tiny body rested in your strong yet gentle arms,
I'd sigh and close my heavy eyes, your proud worn face would beam,
I'd drift away and see my life, you'd be there in every scene.
Your heart held a thousand dreams and your face eternal rest,
Our radiated love with which we bonded was truly blessed,
In the morning you were my first warm ray of light,
And your eyes the twinkling stars last at night.

I'd go to bed early so we could read a tall tale,
If I were poorly a simple hug would make me well,
You'd sit me in the kitchen sink I'd smother you in bubbles,
Getting me to wear modern clothes was double the trouble.
At parties, in plays, parades, the cubs and at school,
You'd make the best costumes I was the envy of all.
The great birthday parties, Sunday roast dinner,
I'd sulk if we'd play and I wasn't the winner.

When I was younger, it was natural to tell you of my hurt and fear,
But it all becomes so complex and expressing yourself is unclear.
I hope I never grow so much that I'm too big to find solace in a hug,
Or too distant to sense your equal need for my company, warm and snug.
Love will never diminish, or rust or fade with years,
But will gain strength from time, laughter, joy and tears.
There will never come an age when I won't think of your gentle touch,
I wish you so may fantastic things as I love you so very much.

Daniel Jones

CHURCHYARD YEW

For centuries I have stood
Silent witness to the seasons,
Slow-growing and unmoving,
Crowned in darkest green.
I have cradled furtive lovers,
Kept their whispered secrets,
Shared their joy at weddings,
At the mystery of birth.
I have felt their hope at Easter,
Benevolence at Christmas,
Joined respectful mourning
As bones return to earth.
I have basked in warmest sunshine,
Braved the harshest winter,
Humoured young boys' folly
As they sought to test my strength.
Still the future beckons,
Full of promise, maybe tears.
I feel the sap of ages rise:
Life force through the years.

Janette Sykes

JEROME (A NEW BORN BABY BOY)

Oh, the beautiful wonder of birth
a new born baby boy
like a portrait painted in happiness
with a soundtrack composed with joy

Nine months to perfection
from head to tiny toes
and shining eyes of wonder
to his little screwed up nose

And so begins the circle
with the turning of the months and years
days of joy and wonder
and sometimes little tears

A special warmly wrapped bundle
cradled, cosy and snug
may his life always be
in the knowledge of God's love

James S Jarvis

HIGHWAY TO HEAVEN

Life is fading, I know not why,
Maybe a place high in the sky,
Is waiting to welcome my aged old limbs,
Can God forgive me, and redress all my sins?

My family long gone, the ones that I cherished,
As my turn arrives I don't really relish,
The thought of eternity for ever more,
Life is so cruel, who knows what's in store?

The years that have passed, have gone quickly by,
With laughter, and humour, and many a cry,
I've lived to the full, and enjoyed my brief life,
Through highways, and byways, in spite of some strife.

Triumphs and failures, some wins, and some losses,
I've even been known to bet on the osses,
You only get out, what you only put in,
So do be realistic, and don't cause a din.

The light is now fading, so low in the sky,
My time is now here, I'm ready to die.
No time left for chapter and verse.
It's final, it's over, for next is the herse.

Michael John Swain

SEASONS AND YOU

The countryside slowly awakens.
Little green plant shoots push through.
I look out upon all the wonders
Of nature and springtime and you.

As the days grow long and warmer
With flowers of beautiful hues.
I see all the warmth and the brightness
Of sunshine and summer and you.

As leaves turn to red, gold and amber
And evenings close in as they do.
The sun still holds warmth in the daytime
For beautiful autumn and you.

Then as the wind whistles around us
With rain, snow and icicles too,
I love all the warmth and the closeness
Of firelight and winter and you.

The year brings such changes in all things.
With skies maybe grey, maybe blue.
But through all, as time swiftly passes
There's love and the seasons and you.

Angela Tomlinson

STAINED

Life extinct at four o'clock
The seconds tick unsolved
Jaws of the onlookers drop
The wife curls up with grief

The ambulance girl turns away
And moves back through the crowd
Another patient lost that day
Her workmates sympathise

Epitaph of accident
Upon the day is stained
With all usual reactions vent
It's forget, work, move on

The pavement that held stiff'ning shell
Its sturdy width unmoved
Cleared back to the innocence
The basis of our lives

Corena J Nicol

LIFE STORY

Standing at her door
daydreaming, the elderly woman
watched the milkman come.
In her wrinkled hands
she held an empty milk bottle.
Just one now, she thought,
like in the early days
when they were first wed;
and then when the baby came
how proudly she'd said
'Two pints today, please'.
Then more babies arrived
and there were five milk bottles.
So the family grew up and
one at a time they left
and the number of bottles
dwindled to just one,
my life, she thought, has been
measured in milk bottles.

Joan Miles Lister

THE CIRCLE

When I was young, I dreamt I'd be
A fairy on a Christmas tree;
My mum and dad would be so pleased
As they gazed up with joy at me.

And when at nine, I learned to tap,
my footwork filled the air
with all the noise that I could make -
and mum, and dad, were there.

Ten years later, and down the aisle,
my dad was at my side;
And when my mum turned in her seat
her eyes filled with pride.

At twenty-two, our child was born,
My cup was overflowing . . .
Our son was lucky to be blessed
with grandparents there, and doting.

The years slipped by, and with them too
went happiness and sorrow -
my dad gave up the will to live,
and mum's visiting tomorrow . . .

My husband, too, he went his way . . .
now mum and I are sitting;
To cover up our discontent
I sew, and she is knitting.

And through the door my grandchild comes -
a pretty girl called Mary;
Grandma, last night I had a dream
I was a Christmas fairy . . .

Marlene White

ON GROWING OLD

There is nothing clever in growing old
Keep living is all you need be told
We, nearly all of us hate the thought
But lotions and potions can be bought
Said to wipe away wrinkles and feed the skin
And massage away a double chin.

As you get older you have to accept
You must slow down and your faculties kept
You have to go slow you cannot be quick
And often you'll need the help of a stick
Old age certainly has limitations
But, thank God, it also has compensations.

Rheumatism, arthritis and aches in the bones
Can make living a misery and life full of groans
As you get older your memory wanes
You'll find more losses than you will of gains
It's when you're young and full of zest,
You usually find you do things best.

Young folk should treat the old with respect,
At least that is something we have come to expect
They should give up their seats on buses for you,
But too often, today, they don't bother to do.
Free prescriptions help to care for your health
And free passes on buses will help with your wealth.

These things and others, will help you to cope
So as you get older don't just give up hope.
It is said we should all of us grow old with grace.
But that is not easy when watching your face.
The best, it is promised, is still yet to be
But I'm afraid that is something I cannot agree.

W M Jones

LIFE - FULL CIRCLE

Life - full circle,
Born into a family,
Warmth and care
And love to share.

Loving - full circle,
A heart that's full
And as you live
So much to give.

Learning - full circle,
On every day,
At every turn
We grow and learn.

Family - full circle,
Children, grandchildren,
Through all the years,
Some smiles, some tears.

Life - full circle,
One life began
And in life's December,
Remember, remember.

Patricia Catling

MOTHER

All her life she tried to please
Mistakes she made were legion
All their pains she tried to ease
All arguments to reason.

Her children grew as children will
And still her love was there
She dried their tears, calmed their fears
And listened to their prayers.

Along came sweethearts, friends and lovers
Some she liked but many others
Faded, when the dreams were ended
And another broken heart was mended.

So now she sits alone at last
Left to contemplate her past
Left to sing her lonely song
Still she wonders
'What went wrong?'

A Stubbs

DEPRESSION

When puzzled thoughts keep racing around
The goldfish bowl of doubts and gloom
Looking for a way out of one's misery
And tossing sleep that cannot come too soon
You do not need 'Come on snap out of it,'
The advice that well meaning relatives lend
But an understanding that this is an illness
That bandages and ointments cannot mend.
Then slowly with good counselling and good company
For one or two hours, happiness shines through,
Which gives you a base that you can build on
With nights out and perhaps a drink or two,
Although at times you may relapse into depression
You know you've been there and conquered it for a while
And so at last with understanding from all around you
Go out with head held high and once more you can smile,
So when you've been through this experience
With no more anti-depressants in your home
You'll understand traumas of the mind that afflict folk
And strengthen them by saying 'You're not alone.'

J B Loader

THE YOUNG LAYABOUT

Shapeless and senseless the day lies ahead,
Why should I bother to get out of bed?
I lie there and wait for the knock on the door,
'What are you lying in bed there for?'

'But if I get up Mum,' I'm wanting to say,
'You know I will only get in your way.'
You bustle around as you tidy and clean,
But I lie and wonder what does life mean?

I'm younger and stronger and fitter than you,
If only I had something worthwhile to do.
'Get down the Job Centre' the grown-ups all say,
But how to explain that's the laugh of the day?

Experience wanted is always the rule,
But how can you have that when you've just left school?
I'll meet my mates later, and sit in a huddle,
But then people think that we're looking for trouble.

Knock, knock on the door, 'Mum give me a break!'
I shout, but really it makes my heart ache.
It's driving me crazy, out of my mind,
If only some meaning to life I could find.

Sally Quinn

BIRDS AND BABIES

Sparrows feeding their young on the garden wall
For seasons I have watched them with joy
But joy no more.
No more I see the gaping beaks the vibrating wings
Now I see a starving baby sucking at a withered breast.

Jackdaws squabbling in the street below
Picking and tearing at a paper bag.
Now silence, they have reached their goal,
Some chips, discarded the night before.
Oh God why, you feed the birds and babies die.
Sure, blame the Lord, he gives us food enough and more,
But we refuse to scatter, we prefer to store.

Owen Murphy

THE YOUNG AND OLD

New on day one all wrinkled and small
old and wiser a teacher that's all.
A time to learn of what is new
a time to teach the things to do.

The touch and look at what it is
to show that life is to exist.
To sit and laugh at having wind
to rub his back to ease the thing.

To cut his teeth which are a pain
to wish that I had mine again.
To learn to walk while being small
these things we learn when we are born.

To run and play and have some fun
to do the things you have done.
At school we learn of right and wrong
and hope we adults don't get it wrong.

Our role in life when we are young
is respect our elders and their love.
Without their teaching where would we be
without their love there would not be me.

Rene

SYMBIOSIS

It's lovely and warm in here, quiet, I get fed on demand
No bright lights I'm on my own
Undisturbed for a few months
Then Blam! I'm shooting through space
Blinding light - then someone slaps me
It's not easy to get nourishment
Discover I can scream and have legs and a brain
Then you're on your own again but in a crowd
You need skill to get what you want
And you have to fight to keep it
Then you start to get tired and wise
And cynical if you're not careful
You forget important details
But remember that woolly rabbit
That hung on a silk thread in your pram
Mummy and daddy have now left you orphaned
You're on your own kid
Suddenly not much is happening
The kids have gone
What's left now is how your body works
This remains the most important topic
Until one day you grow tired of life
And no curiosity remains
Only a biological inevitability
You're on your own kid
Make the most of it.

Julia Wallis-Bradford

SPRING REVERIE

Glories of a morning sky
Set beyond our reach on high
To proclaim to all the world
Wonders of a love unfurled
Shining on us every day
Cheering all our weary way.

Radiance of a summer sun
Giving light to everyone
Rising slowly in the east
Giving warmth to man and beast
Sinking slowly in the west,
Telling all, 'tis time to rest.

Evening skies of sombre hue
And the kiss of morning dew,
Birds' songs at the break of day
And the smell of new-mown hay
Mountains grey with misty light
Capped with snow, so soft and white.

All the sounds of this world
Which around our lives have curled,
All the views our eyes delight -
To those of us with precious sight.
Can we let them pass away -
Without voting Yea or Nay -
To the threatening voice of war
Thus destroying Nature's law?

Marguerite Brassington-Griffiths

HEAVEN'S LIGHT

A small light was all one needed.
She settled down. No other thought,
The light disappeared.

At speed it didn't matter.

It came on. And still she knew.
The light way urged her on and on.
Still no thought came.

She almost fell asleep.

She may have done - for a second or two,
It didn't matter.

The mini bus went on, and on, and on . . .

Ken Round

ONCE

Weary and worn the man hangs his head,
Spent from the climb, his legs turned to lead.
For hours he has toiled up an endless slope
At times he had, almost, given up hope.

Leaning on sticks, he needs their support,
He remembers the times when this was his sport.
When he'd race up peaks, hill after hill,
Feeling endlessly strong, not old, tired and ill.

Now it takes him all day to walk up the street
To the pub on the corner where the pensioners meet.
Together they sit, recalling the days
Before they grew old and mended their ways.

Chris Holder

DREAMS

Our dreams in childhood, wishes too, are hopes and fears
we want anew.
But when we try to change the hate, we can't resolve
what will be fate.
And so beyond a lifetime's needs, are many fantasies
and deeds.
That all too soon we understand and leave behind the
wonderland.
To face reality, and fear to know our destiny is near.
When all is gone then come what may, our hopes and
dreams will always stay,
We need those frailties today to smooth our path
and lead the way.

Edith E Rowell

THANK YOU EMMELINE PANKHURST

Two days ago I was eighteen, the cake has not yet gone,
And now I am about to vote, in the local government election.
I've checked out who is standing, and what they represent,
And I've been guided through the process, by my thoughtful parents.
So thank you Emmeline Pankhurst, and all the others who,
Fought so hard to get the vote for all men and women too.
I'm thinking of you all, as I mark my paper with a cross,
If you hadn't fought for your beliefs, I'd not be here at the ballot box.
Today I've become an adult, I suddenly feel mature,
Voting gives me responsibility, I'm helping to shape our future.
I'll never forget the struggles, of Emmeline and all the rest,
And at every future election, I'll be there to put my cross.

Cathy Houghton

MY TRIBUTE

With a heart nearly broken it isn't easy to write. Not easy to narrate about words spoken during long years of pain and tears, but I am proud to be able to mention the courage of my late wife. I will be for the rest of my life.

She was an ordinary person I suppose. Never noticed in a crowd but her smile was as sweet as any rose and despite her suffering, her pain, she'd hardly ever complain. Life is for today she would say. For hours and hours I sat with her, through the tears and sorrow. Through nights that seemed like years I watched her body becoming more ravaged. She never ever mentioned tomorrow for fate had become more unkind, more cruel, attacking even her mind. Stripping it bare. In some terrible moments of despair when she ached from head to foot I would take her in my arms, comfort her. Christ it wasn't fair.

Sometimes I would have to leave the room and wipe a tear filled eye, then when she asked 'Is everything alright?' I'd lie, then take her in my arms, silently praying for the Lord to help her, to dispel the pain, the fear and qualms. She needed God - and me so much and I would touch her face, her hands, her hair. Tell her how much I loved her. I was always there. I would fiddle with the gold band that was now slipping from her finger. I'd talk about old times, down a lane of memories linger. Sometimes I would cry because I noticed liquid dribbling from her mouth because she'd forgotten how to swallow. She'd look at me with sad troubled eyes and I'd wallow in self pity knowing the end was near. Just before it happened her speech was slurred and she would try to ask me 'What's wrong, am I going to die?' and with blurred eyes from crying again I'd lie and try to be strong. My poor darling has gone now but there is one extra special moment that will forever be in my mind. She bade me near her, kissed me and with a voice I could hardly hear, said 'Thanks for looking after me. For being so kind'. This is my tribute brave lady. My last salute. 'Lord hold her near.'

Frederic Davies

THE LAST RESTING PLACE

Looking over the graveyard neat
People sleeping beneath our feet,
In Westminster Abbey or under the sod
It doesn't matter when you're going to God,
He doesn't judge you on the place you're laid
Or on how much money you made.
You won't have to run another race
When you come to the final resting place.

June Hipwell

LIVING SEED

I am a tiny little seed
Provided free with all I need
Rainwater's my favourite drink
Not from the tap as some folk think
And soil's all I need to eat
Freshly dug you cannot beat
Soon I'll grow, my skin will break
And a long white root I'll make
A green shoot will come from the top
And through the soil I will pop
My shoot will unfurl
Scarlet petals, lovely smell
My life gives pleasure I can tell
But soon life's finest hours fade
And sadly decay will invade
But all's not lost 'cause life won't die
My life has gone, but please don't cry
'Cause through my life new seeds are born
And will give you joy one fresh new morn.

Wendy Dedicott

AS TURNS THIS SWIFT WHEEL

Is life a circle, recurrent and thriving,
Where did it all start . . . .?
It is, one may argue, perpetual motion
Brought to a fine art . . .
That tiny beginning, a marvel in prospect
Enlarged day by day,
So soon through to manhood, when age drives relentless
Till death calls away.
And is there a purpose . . . ? And will there be ending
As turns this swift wheel . . .?
For life is so earnest, with some . . .incorporeal . . .
Spiritually real.

Mute nature unprejudiced, like an incumbent,
Has no thought of time . . .
Beginning or ending . . . she suffers each season
In patience sublime;
But with Homo Sapiens, restless, uncertain,
The great question . . . why . . .?
Who measures existence, where light-years defeat him,
Within his vast sky!
That Power, long controlling, alone knows the answer
To what, why and when,
Who promises life until ends this fair epoch,
Revealing all then;
'Tis ours but to live to the full in our orbit
Around a blithe sun,
Grateful in heart our sweet span is unchanging
Since time was begun.

The Warwickshire Poet

SPRINGTIME

The earth is waking up again
Now that springtime's here
With the warmth and with the rain
The plants will re-appear

The yellow trumpet daffodils
Sway gently in the breeze
The bluebells of the forest
Ring softly 'neath the trees

The gold and purple crocuses
Form blankets on the ground
And everywhere you look
New beginnings can be found

The little robin redbreast
Flies to and fro in haste
To build a comfy nest
His time he must not waste

The cuckoo will return
And soon we'll hear its song
She'll lay her eggs in another bird's nest
Then she'll be moving on

As we say farewell to winter
And herald in the spring
It's such a joy to see
New life in everything.

Linda Boon

HOW DO YOU KNOW YOU'RE HERE?

How do you know you're here my friend?
Perhaps your really not!
No one's ever proved we are,
No one's proved we're not.
From the oldest inhabitant,
To the kiddy in the cot,
No one knows the answer,
When, why, what;
No one knows the answer,
I doubt they ever will,
The question's a disturbing one,
I fear the answer's more disturbing still?
Time may give us the answer.
As the years go by,
Of how we came to be here,
If we are, and why!

Brian Slade

COSTING THE DEARTH

The hurt is not borne without cost;
As you say: I am stronger than you.
You know not, the days I have lost
When your words, to me, are not true.
I know how to deal with the loss,
And I drown the pain with red wine
And pretend I don't give a toss
When I know you are spinning a line.
On days when the skies weep for me
And I wait with my dearly bought hope;
I hide want, so you cannot see,
Nurse my ache - Oh yes, I can cope.

Marianne Elliott

DAY DREAMS

I feel so good, I think I could fly,
I run around, I shout, I jump so high,
Football and cricket
I'm last in the wicket,
Boxing and climbing,
I hear bells chiming.
In the playground playing at tig,
Running and falling laughing and calling,
Everything looks so big.
The world is a pleasure, so happy and gay,
Each day is a treasure, in every way,
There's a knock at the door,
I try to jump from my chair,
But I cannot move, without the stick that lays there,
I'm old I realise oh so fast,
They were just daydreams
From my long distant past.

Eddie Ingram

TO REFLECT . . .

The spiral of life drifting upwards
Time progressing infinitely onwards
Reflection upon simple childhood days
Seems cloudy in my mind, as my memory frays
Teenage years cars, girls, 'n beers
Acne, school and sexual fears
Middle age, marriage, kids, home, 'n car
Each memory has its scar
These ages mould, to make me who I am
A child no longer, I've become an old man
Retrospect shows me time goes by so fast
I've got my future to enjoy 'n now I've got my past . . .

John Graham

MY LITTLE GIRL

I ache deep within my womb
for the little girl I never had.
A little girl,
yours and mine
to love,
a product of our love.
My arms ache
to hold this little girl,
my arms ache
to hold you
and the love we never
consummated,
but I know deep, deep down
inside
should have been.

Angela Patchett

REQUIEM FOR PETER

Since I can no longer look
Into the depths of your calm eyes,
Nor watch you frown or grin with glee
At some ambiguous surprise;

Since I shall never know again
The comfort of your hand's warm touch,
Nor hear you laugh, with me for foil,
That made me still behave as such;

These gone, I yet will be your love,
And seek through all the realms of space
The soul whose call is clearer still,
Robbed of your voice and face.

Joan King

THE OLD MAN

The old man sits alone, his wrinkled face aglow with smile
Eyes closed, he is lost in dreams that linger for the while
The sands of time are running out in the upturned hour glass
Jaded memories of his youthful days with deliberation pass.

Outside the tempest wind against the shuttered window blows
The old man sits oblivious of time, as the open fire glows
Along the path of long gone youth he slowly makes his way
There in dreams he relives again the memories of yesterday.

His body now with effort moves responsive to his dreams
Boyish voices shout with glee, maidens vent their screams
Mischievous is the smile upon his face as he slumbers on
A subdued sigh passes through his lips then suddenly is gone.

Does it matter if the old man awakes no more
Has he not done the tasks in life that he was destined for
In peaceful rest let him escape the pains that come with age
And from this book of life, let him relive each memorable page.

Arthur Saunders

JOBCENTRE

I'd be a chef but I can't cook
A fashion designer if I could find that look
I'd be a barmaid if I had a taste for rum
A model if I had a smaller bum
I'd be a doctor but I can't stand blood
A nun, but I'm not always good
I'd be a dancer but I've got two-left feet
A fire-fighter if I could stand the heat
I'd be an actress but I couldn't stand the pain
I'd be a lifeguard but my skin would get all wrinkly
A refuse person but I'd be a bit stinky.

Sarah Armstrong

TODAY

Crumbled bones are all that's left
Of a body which once was strong.
The time to die is drawing near;
Oh, where did I go wrong?

I tried and tried to put things right,
But I didn't know what to do -
I prayed to God for a little help
And bones that felt like new.

If I could have my time again
I now know what I'd say;
I wouldn't try to look ahead,
'I'll live just for today.'

Christine McNaught

IN A WEAK MOMENT

In a weak moment, I had one today,
I thought of 'himself', he would not go away,
A friend, she had seen him, and she told me she had,
My stomach felt funny, my heart became sad.
I pretend I don't care, but we all know the truth.
My heart was broken, I'm barely living proof.
But feeling like I do, it isn't like living,
My tears are there, but no, I'm not giving.
But in a weak moment, I'll sit myself down,
And grieve for him, my face wears a frown,
and in a weak moment for myself I'm upset,
For the 'man' that I lost, and the man I can't get,
and in a weak moment I'll write it all down,
as the tears smudge the ink and the letters all drown.

Hannah Mew

COUNTING THE BLESSINGS

In the permanent twilight of autumn
Beneath swiftly de-clad trees
And nearly-naked branches
Where rain drips from stubborn - hung leaves,
The half-light is truly deceptive
With its late - autumnal glow
And I believe in the magic seasons
And the promise of each day we know
Yet, a stray thought lurks on the horizon
And sweeps from the sea to the shore,
Of lands far away 'cross the ocean
Where autumn brings fear to the poor.
So their tears mingle with the raindrops,
Or freeze in the cold of the snow,
And bellies are swollen with hunger,
War and want may be all they will know.
Count your blessing with each welcome harvest
And the fire in the hearth all aglow,
For compared to some in our vast world
We've abundance of food to bestow.

Wendy P Frost

SUICIDE NOTE

It's raining.
My wife has left me.
The dog died.
The bank rang.
There's nothing on TV.
I didn't get invited to the party.
I lost my job.
Goodbye.

Alison Jacobs

THE MOURN IS IN MOURNING

The mourn through Strabane is mourning the dead,
Its waters deliquescent, is but a requiem instead,
Vaporising incense, climbing high to the sky,
Recalls assassinations, so recently plied.
Spirits intertwined with light echoes of mist,
Fleetingly, prancingly, then they are missed.
Consciences are pricked, preserved in the quick.
Anniversaries, in the chronicle, deeply missed, is in print,
While loving memory, in the weekly, sadly missed, is reviewed,
The living so sublime, compassion bereft,
Did pilot wash his hands in the liquid of mourn?
Granting right to the armalite, chasing backwards in time.
History floods through Strabane, to the Finn, to the Foyle
And the Foyle with the Boyne to mix with alanticism, as in Yore.
Wilson, Knox Polk and Dunlap on the shore, await with advice,
'Sort out your own gore.'
Clean minds, fresh looks, black propaganda abounds,
Low achievers, those misplaced, hardmen hang around.
The youth is the future, was not Milton so blind,
To leave paradise lost to the thieves of our time.

Patrick McCourt

THOUGHTS ON THE DAY THE LAST ONE LEFT HOME

There's hot water in the bathroom -
No footsteps on the stair,
No cry 'Where's my tie?
I'm late - I'll not get there'

The kitchen sits there - tidy -
Clock ticking on the wall,
'Where's my jumper - you've got mine!'
No, not that at all.

No sandwiches to prepare
No uniform to press
No broken hearts to be mended -
No bedrooms in a mess.

This is the whole new life then -
The life that is all mine
But no one told me how I start,
Especially at half past nine!

Jean Allison

MODERN LIFE

This modern life, with all its modern ways
This chap's not old, yet still prefers earlier days.

A world of buttons and anti-glare screens
Where cash and personal service are becoming has-beens.

Where mechanical voices reply to a telephone call
Maximum profits remain the be all and end all.

Where work is as rare as a house with a view
And Giro Collectors form an orderly queue.

Where chemical rivers flow in safe legal limits
Yet misshapen fish lay caught in these over-fished nets.

The old soldier lies beaten in yet another mindless attack
Wartime relic hidden, so close . . .
If only modern law allowed him to fight back.

So don't look for excuses or someone to blame
Because in this modern life there's only more of the same.

Andrew Bridges

THE FLEDGLINGS

There is a memory in my heart
of when I walked on air -
When all the birds sang
just for me -
no feeling can compare.

My arms were filled with
softness sweet, pure, all
mine and new -
To feel and see the wonder of
the miracle of you.

Now time's moved on,
the cradle's bare.
No toys are on the floor -
one thing's unchanged -
My love for you, I couldn't
love you more.

There are two young ladies
in this world -
Their adult lives quite new -
And all the blessings in
my heart - I give to both of you.

I keep within the cupboard
old souvenirs, quite worn -
but in my heart are memories
of the day you both were born.

Vanessa Hulme

NO NEED FOR WORDS

You give them life. They bring you joy
With loving care you raise them
And even though they can annoy
When they succeed you praise them
You are so happy on their wedding day
Your heart is full of pride
As they take their vows and kneel to pray
Beside their pretty bride
Grandchildren you then adore
All loved as were your own
Who learn to treasure even more
All the blessings you have shown
So now as time is fading fast
They sit beside your bed
Remembering the joyful past
As they stroke your loving head
An understanding gentle touch
A smile sweet and sincere
For someone you love very much
As you brush away a tear
Although no word is spoken
Your actions speak for you
They will know by this small action
That you are sincere and true
A look that says I love you
Can mean more than any word
All barriers it will break through
Though not a sound is heard.

D Davis

49

OF LOVE AND ETERNITY

We've been together since the dawn of time,
kissed in ebony skies.
I've danced with you at creation's edge,
watched the first moon rise in your eyes.
Lit your starless nights
with the bloodthreaded light
of the tears from lightning years
which painted your silhouette
in the infinite depth
of shadow colours
no rainbows ever known
as I sang to you in times haunting tune
that men try to call their own.
The oath that we swore
still bears the scars,
married to the blood that dripped
from opened wrists
to foetal hearts.
In the paraselene
of a rebirthed dream,
we'll still be together,
dancing forever,
beyond the end of time,
when the aureole of all eternity crowns, the last moon as it
darkly shines.

Alene Kimm

ALWAYS

I was, I am and will always be,
A stream of light that comes from thee;
I had, I have and know to come,
All waves of life flow into one.

What was is now, and now will be,
For all I am is part of me,
No past, no present future time,
I was and will be always thine.

Alexis E Pritchard

THE ROSE OF JERICO

Of all the flowers God made to grow,
Let us cherish the rose of Jerico,
It blossoms and dies till the skies give rain,
Then, it comes to life and blooms again!

In Jerico, our saviour walked
And as he walked, he talked and talked,
Telling of the end of misery and strife,
Saying: 'I am the way, the truth and the life!'

The way that he taught was God's own way,
The truth was the words God told him to say,
The life was the everlasting kind
Fit for a man with a perfect mind!

God, he said to Daniel: 'Go forward to the end;
You will stand up for your lot some day!' on this, he could depend.
When heaven meets the earth and the healing waters flow
And the deserts are all blooming like the rose of Jerico!

And so this perfectly lovely bloom
Radiates hope for me in my room,
For, I lost a loved one and I miss him so!
Want us both to live forever like the rose of Jerico!

Catherine Flint

VE DAY '95

In life's rotund biography
True love survives soul deep
So espying sweet young lovers
Beelzebub feigns sleep
Concocting conflagrations
While sorrowful seraphs weep

But Eros is artful
Waylaying all woes
Encapturing rapture
In ethereal throes
What devils divide
The gods juxtapose

Thus years after parting
Lost letters - won war
Surprised they stumble
Together once more
Skeletons may tumble
But love conquers all.

Angela Simpkin

LANCASHIRE LIFE PAST AND PRESENT

Owd Lancashire, in t'past,
'Wer mooer,
Cotton mills, un Coal mines,
An' Tha knows
'Folk wer gin
Ration books, Coupons
Alus towd
Mak um last
Till recession wer thrivin gain.

Life in Lancashire nowadays,
Everything easily acquired.
Money doesn't seem to stretch far
As VAT on most items required
Microchips overtake hard labour
Computers' knowledge
Folks' infinite time saviour.

Patricia Firth

LIFE

Life is like the water cycle
Born with the rain it enters into its own small streams
Made up of small family groups.
Slowly and without any real warning.
You are swept into a river,
Full of bigger 'groups'
Startling as this is, you can still retain some individuality.
With even less of a warning than previously,
We are flung out into the 'sea of life'.
To become unrecognisable, simply tolerated
To be a part of a whole, part of one moving expanse
To face trials and tribulations.
To face the crisis point of life riding on the crest of a wave.
Only to make it inseparable, indistinguishable,
from anything else after the crash
To be no more
Finally after paying your tribute, making your contribution,
You are summoned to the skies to receive your due on whether you will go
up
or
down.

F Kauser

IT WAS ON A STARRY NIGHT ...

The road seems oh so bumpy
The stars are shining bright
Slow down, you say quite breathless
I think we'll have all night!
Finally you get there
You wobble through the door
Collapse into a wheelchair
They're coming more and more
OK - this is it - no escape for you
You touch your lump quite fondly
But it hurts you through and through
Maybe in half an hour
Maybe in just a week
Another breath of gas and air
Your partner's hand you seek
Soon it will be over
And you will gently touch
What was the bump inside you
You've wanted, oh so much . . .

Belinda Woodcock

A LONELY HEART

She sat on the seat as cold as could be.
     Her hands were as blue as the mysterious sea.
The smile on her face was no longer there.
     Her heart was like stone but nobody cared.
Where had they all gone? The people she knew.
     The ones she had loved, there had been quite a few.
But no use to them now, she no longer could be.
     So she sat all alone by the mysterious sea.

Sybellena Bridge

TO DIE

Life itself is the biggest lie of all
in the end, what have we achieved?
We're dying since the day we first learnt to crawl,
a contradiction to what we've believed.

Then death is the end, but an end to what?
Of suffering and heartache and pain?
Is death the beginning of all that life was not
or will man be born once again?

When life is through with tormenting your soul,
does death do for eternity the same?
Or if you did not quite reach your life's goal
do you come back to finish the game?

Under six-feet of earth in a cold web of death,
in eternal nothingness; blank.
Then why is man so scared to draw his last breath,
for in death all are equal in rank.

Is death the twilight hour of our life,
the dark before the new day?
A few moments of rest from worries and strife,
before you continue on your way.

Yet death is among us from birth to end,
as we watch our life's years slip us by.
For death is the cure for all ills, my friend,
so tell me, are you scared to die?

P J Houghton

TRAMPLED UNDERFOOT

Upon arrival to this commercialised jungle,
Your first course of survival is destined to begin in a cradle.
The given growing time
And though peace of mind,
Mental and physical progression
Are assembled in rhyme;
And soon you exchange your cradle or a school satchel.
From whence, you're forced to adjust
To a lifestyle that lacks the common sense of inner trust.
When you become more attuned to life,
You're taught how to be righteous husband and wife,
And all the correct rituals to a good life.
Then you have to face life at one and every angle, but honestly,
Where does your arse really dangle?
For most leave programmed to receive and most are openly received
To live through life without much ever being achieved;
Then you leave!

Dave White

TIME PASSING

If I could sail on one more tide
Or climb another mountainside
The joy of youth I would know again
And still be striving to attain
Fulfilment of the impossible dream
All earth's wonders to have seen

Southern sea and silver shore
Rugged headland rocky tor
Calling me to explore
Just one more time just one time more.

Deep the yearning and the longing
Sad the knowing time has gone,
Fireside slippers now for me
Easy chair and memory.

Goodbye to mountain's furrowed face
Goodbye to nature's wild embrace
For time the healer, time the stealer
Is time the winner of the race.

Margaret B Copeman

LIFE TOGETHER

I saw him round the neighbourhood,
Never spoke to him, perhaps I should.
Casually we met in the street
And decided that we should have to meet.

Started dating every night,
Walking and talking in the moonlight.
We didn't want ever to part,
It was real true love from the start.

The wedding bells began to chime,
Then I knew that he was mine.
A new life started for both of us
As we finished the day with a fuss.

Three years of happy bliss,
The news of a baby was sealed with a kiss.
A few years later a second baby, what a treat,
It certainly made our family complete.

Thirty seven years of ups and downs,
But our love was stronger we found.
Then one day fate stepped in,
Took you away and left me lonely and grim.

Evelyn M Harding

SORROW

Her dad died when she was but a child.
The memory of that day still fixed and retained
and flashbacks bring back sorrow and pain
On her dad's face was pain
as he clutched at his chest
he changed his clothes as he gasped for breath
Her heart was breaking as she felt the fear
of losing the dad she held so dear.
Something was wrong
a feeling of dread
she felt it, she knew it her father was dead.
Don't say it mam she screamed in her head
dont say it mam don't say he's dead.
Her heart raced faster
a lump in her throat
the impeding disaster please God, I hope, *no*
Her mam crumpled and slumped on the bed
I'm sorry love, but daddy is dead.
It had come true
the heartbreaking news
her worse fears, her nightmare
her life was confused.
The one she loved was dearly taken away
but the pain she feels gets less
day by day
'Til memories bring them back to the fore
and the pain starts again
for a little while more.

J Williams

I WISH

I wish, I were a child again
A playful lad I'd be
With lots of toys and bric-a-brac
To play with endlessly.

To parade my troops before the guns
The general, I am he,
And order them to battle in all their finery.

Oh, wish I were a child again
What games there were to play
Chap the door and runaway
Marbles, conkers, hide and seek.

To be the king of the castle
With Curs and Varlaits at my feet
Or the captain of a pirate ship
In sail of adventures yet to meet.

Alas these days are long since gone
An adult, I am he,
With no toys or bric-a-brac
Only endless drudgery.

My memories are a medicine
To combat this malady
So I'll open my book of past pages
Before it's time for tea.

To run for fun towards a setting sun
With my friends of yesterday
I'd do it all tomorrow, to be a child again.

Michael John McKernan

RIVER OF LIFE

We are being swept along by the river of life,
From the moment of our birth.
Through turbulent rapids, which we call strife,
'Til we reach the calmer seas of this earth.

If we are lucky, we are born in the calm;
Of a household full of love.
Where caring parents guard us from harm,
And all's right with our world, as in heaven above.

But into this life some rain must fall.
We can't live all the time in the sun.
We must learn to paddle our own canoe,
And to do what we are taught to do.

The ocean of life is a tumultuous place,
With whirlpools and big waves to throw us off course.
As though trying to drown the entire human race;
But there's still a much more powerful force.

Our creator who made this dangerous sea,
Also made lifebelts for you and for me.
They're called family and friends, here to help one another,
From the day of our birth 'til our journey ends.

And when our river of life is o'er,
We will find it has swept us for evermore;
To a higher plane, way above this world,
Where the mysteries of life will be unfurled.

When our own river has run its course,
We'll be swept along by this greater force;
Then gently guided on a placid sea,
To a calm, safe harbour for eternity.

Jean M Senior

THE LORE OF LIFE

Somewhere on my mind's un-dusted shelf
Knickknacks of knowledge un-touching delve.
Must I blow away the dust and remove the temporal strife,
Pluck from the indifferent air the dawn and dusk of life?
Teach me not to see with un-answering eyes
But contemplate without malice, and draw breath without lies.
For the meaning of being is hidden inside
The unfathomed depth of knowing to be taken with stride.
Teach me to consider with the passing of time
The flamboyance of curves - the dullness of lines.
The institute of life with its yielding passion,
Its measured habit and soulful fashion.
The celebration of life, the ritual of death
Save I should take my final breath.

Sally Colgate

SHATTERED DREAMS

This yearning deep inside me, has always been a part,
Of all the hopes and fears, that I hold within my heart.
People think it is easy, they offer their advice,
'How long have you been married? A baby would be nice.'

They do not know the reasons, they never stop to think,
That we cannot have children, and we have reached the brink.
Our dreams have all been shattered, our hopes are all torn down,
We made the sky the limit, but in this sea we drown.

We try to swim to safety, the current seems so strong,
And as the waves awash us, we try to struggle on.
It never will be easy, no matter what they say,
But we will gain in strength, and the scars will fade away.

Veronica McCaughey

MARRIAGE BLESSING
JULY 23RD 1994

A glorious day - the scene was set
At All Saints Church the family met.
A marriage blessing for Jenni and Jon
His Australian bride and our handsome son.
The scent of roses drifted around
To the altar they came without a sound
Only a smile and a tear from Mum
'A beautiful service; agreed everyone

Out in the sunshine for camera poses
Reminders and memories for future enclosures
Joyful reunions for young and old
His bride to be welcomed into the fold
Adjourn to the Golf Club - reception time
Everyone chatting and drinking wine
The speeches were excellent Jon made us smile
with his Aussie accent and humorous style

A four piece band played all night long
with a break for Jon to sing a song
Guitar in hand rendering Johnny B Good
He brought the house down, knew he would.
Goodbyes and good luck as guests finally depart
We share our son's happiness with love in our heart
The stars shone bright as they drive away
A perfect ending to a perfect day.

Jenny Hornsey

REJECTED ONE

To the one whom I rejected,
So many years ago.
The love I feel for you now,
You will never know.

Much sorrow we both have known,
Such sadness of the heart.
And my, how the years have flown
Since we were torn apart.

We weren't meant to be together,
That is my belief.
Not meant to comfort one another,
Or share each other's grief.

Tragedy did strike in both our lives,
The experiences differ.
But if I had become your wife,
Things may have turned out better.

Now we are both middle-aged,
Our paths may cross again,
And happiness could be our wage.
I wish I knew just when!

I am Aries, you are Libra,
Both go well together.
'Twas my mistake rejected one,
To have left you for another.

Pat Drew

MOTHERHOOD

After a long wait we finally met each other,
From that moment I became her mother,
In another my life changed and I changed,
As my exhausted body recovered from labour pain,
Two new-born eyes opened and gazed at me,
Suddenly I saw the future and how it would be,
In the commitment of our forth coming years,
I would wipe her nose and dry her tears,
I would be a singer of nursery rhymes,
An artist of felt tip and crayoned lines,
A teacher, teaching her all of life's facts,
An entertainer with many different acts,
I would guide her as she made her way through life,
Until she became a woman and maybe a wife,
Then one day she may also become a mother,
But I will still be hers and I'll always love her.

Kathleen Speed

LIFE WITHOUT PURPOSE

The winds of death flapped silently
Around the rooms of the small house
Its cold breath rising above the heat of the log fire.
In one corner sat the oak coffin
Large and inhospitable amidst the worn
Carpet and cheap trinkets,
Tears marked the woman's face
Staining each wrinkle without preference
Everything seems so quiet now
So empty without purpose
Turning again to the coffin she sobbed deeply
Not for the present, nor for her dead lover
But for the future with no meaning.

Paul Gray

JUST A CHILD

Being a child isn't all that much fun, with grownups telling you,
how thing should be done.
Speak when your spoken to - is one that I hate, and 'Leave your knife
and fork side by side on your plate'
Sit round, face the table - don't gobble your food. I don't want my friends
to think you are rude.
Come when I call you, where have you been?
Why can't you keep your new dress nice and clean.
Have you washed your hands - just look at your face, and you've not
combed your hair - it's all over the place.
Why don't you listen, I've told you before - you must not leave toys on
The Living Room Floor.

Well - I know when I grow up I'm going to see that I don't treat my
children - the way mum treats me.

Norma C Crone

FORGETFULNESS

F   Forever and a day my dear
O   Our love will stay with me.
R   Remember? It is just a year
G   God plucked you from the sea.
E   Each day I want to join you love
T   Together we will be,
F   Forever and a day my love,
U   Until Eternity.
L   Lean down from there and cuddle me.
N   No longer will I cry
E   Each night I need you close to me;
S   So pray to God I die.
S   Six years ago it was he drowned.

Evelyn Golding

HONEYCOMBED

Layers of frothy petticoats
Rounded out
beneath a full-skirted Linzi dress a-flouncing
Dolcis winkle-picker
stepping feet
I'm toe-pinched ready for the dancing
Bouffant hairstyle
beehive fashion
teased from silken tresses flowing
lacquered a-la-pompadour fragrant
in perfumed clouds of Blue Grass scent
my face creme-puffed and glowing
All set for jazz club jiving
Coffee bar hiving
Smooching to RCA records of Elvis Presley
he of the lips
swivel hips
Rockin'n'rolling - kingly he impressed me.
Fluttering petty notes
scattered out
fragrant leaves of salad-days - girlish fun romancing
Brownie-box snapshots
slipper my feet
toes pinch at the thought of all that dancing.
Where would we be without reminiscence
these buzzing sweet cells of golden memory's bloom
mine are nestling within
my photograph album
a treasured time-zone - honeycombed.

Lucy Green

WHERE ARE YOU?

We used to call him 'Danny Boy'
He filled our life with love and joy
We marvelled at how fast he grew
So quick the days of youth they flew.

Then one day he was not there
We could not find him anywhere
He vanished like the melting snow,
Wherever did our darling go.

I look into the grown up face
But can't see the slightest trace
He looks at me with stranger's eyes
And deep within me something dies.

My heart calls out in mute despair,
My son, dear son, are you in there?
But he kept his distance, far away
From the loving child of yesterday.

It happens oft' that with the years,
A little child just disappears
That lovely lad who once was ours
Has vanished like the summer flowers.

We never saw the shadow creeping
It beckoned him and left us weeping
We turned around and he had gone
Like the dew from the lawn

The world had called and he had grown
For such a little time we own
Those clinging hands and trusting ways
So soon are gone those childhood days.

Thomas Boyle

CIRCLE OF LIFE

Two people meet - they fall in love
This is determined from above.

So begins the circle of our life
Girl meets boy - becomes a wife.

Days of joy and eager greeting
Happiness is felt at each meeting.

Comes the day they decide to wed
Following on this - comes the nuptial bed.

Or at least - this was so - you must agree
Nowadays it is let's try and see!

Then comes the time to know each other
There may come a time when there's a sister and brother.

The days go by - then months and years
During this time there may be laughter and tears.

It is said we should learn from trouble and strife
Why is it some people have a troublesome life?

Of course, there are some whose troubles they hide
Others get relief by not keeping things inside.

How often we hear of families so 'together'
Who go through life quietly in stormy weather.

How can we tell why we are here
Perhaps if we knew - we'd be full of fear.

Yet man believes there is a hereafter
When we will live happily ever after.

We get older, slow down - regret the passed years
We try not to fear how long we may have left - knowing our loved ones will be
bereft.

So let's make the most of what we are allowed
So that our circle of life wont be hidden in a shroud.

Sheila Mozelman

AMBITIONS IN LIFE
(For my friends)

Life is full of good, bad, terrible and evil things
Life is full of school, college, homework and engagement rings
But what about our ambitions, what we want and care for
The future for example, or a world wide tour.
What about the things our ancestors set
     so we could change and try to put
     Right
We can try as hard as superman, we can try
     with all our might.
We can bring back now a person on the
     verge of death
When they think they have breathed their
     very last breath.
But what about animals, some killed cruelly
     some killed with care
What makes some people think this is fair
We can change the world for the better if we
     try
Instead of giving the future generation a
     pillow on which to cry!

S Rashid (14)

A SHRED OF LIME GREEN

He rings on the doorbell
sends songs on a tape.
Draws through mist on a window,
February's valentine's shape.
The answerphone winking
a shred of lime green
which cuts like glass
through the bedlam of dreams.
Crumple the paper,
Tear up the scrawl,
of spiralling letters
on the shelf in the hall.
Throw out the snap-shots
of two holidays past.
Pack away the album
Where only illusion can last.

J A Lawrence

NEW BORN

Cradled in my arms,
while generations of relations
crowd in upon your being,
seeing, with consummated longing,
the bands of belonging.
Linked through time,
an unbroken line
of inheritance and survival,
renewed by your arrival.
Within you lies the core
of all that went before
and is yet to be.
Bold whisper of eternity.

Shirley Johnson

THE LIFE CYCLE

First you worry, then you wonder
That babies so small can survive.
Yet, soon their spell, you are under,
As every ruse they contrive.

Your concern as they develop;
Interest at every stage.
In your love you, them, envelop;
Firm guidance give them as they age.

Your own life widens as they learn;
Their fears and hopes for you to share.
You may not know for all they yearn;
Then trust will bind your loving care.

The age they seem most defiant,
Is time for courting - leaving home -
To spread wings - be self-reliant;
Testing time for trust, as they roam.

As they quickly age, so do you;
The cycle - birth to parenthood -
Constantly - old gives way to new;
You would not change it if you could.

That is how life on earth does go;
First you learn, then move on to teach.
You take the lead, help others grow,
'Til own maturity they reach.

Now in old age you have your part;
In busy life they keep in touch;
Your guidance still within each heart;
Your support welcomed very much.

A great - grandchild sleeps in my arms,
So contented - for, all, she charms.

Roy Hammond

A WOMAN'S LIFE

(The baby)   Mirror mirror
                    Tell the story
                    Downy skin
                    Wide wondering eyes.

(The child)   On the wall
                    Glance in passing
                    Tangled hair
                    And grubby face.

(The Teenager) Who is fairest?
                    You at this age.
                    Grasp at life,
                    Take all it gives

(The bride)   Of them all
                    This day will bring
                    Sweet memories
                    Throughout the years.

(The mother)   You are fair,
                    The pregnant glow
                    Full of promised
                    Life to come.

(The widow)   But she is fairer
                    Far than you
                    Who've lost a love
                    A need to be.

(Old age)   Snow-white is
                    Your once black hair
                    Mother's eyes
                    Return your stare

(Death)	Smash and splinter
	Break the mould.
	Reflections weep
	When we get old.

Alfreda Ballad

JOURNEY

You came into the world,
A slippery, slimy serpent of a thing,
Which turned into a rotund baby,
Mouth constantly open,
Looking for succour.

By the time you were five
your indomitable spirit, became apparent,
Innumerable times,
You fell off your two wheeler,
To pick yourself up again,
Staunchly refusing to have the
wheel balancers put back on.

Crowned at ten with a silver tiara,
How we wished we'd called you
Just plain Sarah,
You held your superior nose up high,
And a dreamy look came in your eyes.

Now your suitcase is packed in the hallway,
A law unto your own,
Do you think you can make the journey,
Into womanhood all alone?

Elizabeth Carne

CIRCLES OF LIFE - REINCARNATION

As circles of life move round and round
Vague lost memories are sometimes found.
Perhaps it's some person, place or sound
Which reawakens that well trod ground.

As fleeting images dance into view
Familiar shapes, perspective askew.
Are these odd remnants of something new?
Or the uneasy happenings of dè já vu?

Life turns for most of us too fast.
Fading colours hang from the mast.
As spinning wheel from present to past,
Delivers that ball and the die is cast.

Footprint recollections erased from the shore.
Hindsight forbidden to alter the score.
Flickering images through the revolving door
Remind us no less, but help us no more.

And as we can't those past lives span
Neither alter; nor our destinies plan.
With the little help that given to man,
He's to worklife through as best he can.

H D Hensman

LIFE'S CLOCK

As I listen to the clock, ticking away,
So peaceful, it almost, sends me to sleep.
Again, I listen, in silence, as the noise,
Fills the room, with a regular beat.

This is my life, ticking away,
Quietly, urgently, passing in time.
It is the present, then the past, slipping so fast,
Never stopping, keeping in rhyme.

Should the clock, of our life, stop, or break down,
All life, would come to halt,
Past and present, would merge, and be as one,
Who would repair the fault?

Is there a craftsman, who can repair life's clock?
Or, is the future, in the hands of the Gods?
Does life's clock, beat, until eternity itself?
Never ending, until all life stops.

Shirley Thompson

OWT FOR NOWT

The sign which read *admission free*
Aroused my curiosity
Having nothing else to do
I waited in the winding queue

Would there be some famous writer
Or perhaps a champion fighter
Who would turn away and laugh
When I begged an autograph

Or someone from a magazine
Demonstrating *haute cuisine*
Impatiently with breath abated
I tried to find out why we waited

At three the doors were opened wide
With mouth agape I looked inside
There resplendent in array
The bloomers I had thrown away

So heed the moral of this tale
Or end up at a *jumble sale*

Lillian Conway

DEAR ANNIE

It's sixty years Dear Annie
Since I left you in this grave
Fond memories of you I carry
Even till this day

Sixteen you were when we were wed
How happy you made me feel
Short lived was my happiness
When death took you from me

I could not except our parting
Or settle in, what we called home
I thought I'd make a life anew
and take another road

The road I took was America
To join my brother John
I left my parents and country
But you I took along

I worked and lived in the city
Its tall buildings and broad streets
I made a lot of acquaintances
nice people I was blessed to meet.

But no maiden could hold my feelings,
No one could take your place
There is not a day that I live through
That I don't behold your face.

I am back now, Dear Annie
Old and in failing health
My days I'm told are shorter
My days on earth near spent,

Yet I'm looking forward to our meeting
In the heavens high above
To the God that brings us together
In his eternal love.

Stephen Paul McCann

LITTLE FRIEND
(A poem for my son)

Into the world he came
my innocent little child.
This boy I'd helped create,
worth the tiresome wait.

With loving helpless eyes,
this boy looks up to me.
An image of pure perfection,
longing for my protection.

My nervous loving eyes
watch proudly as he grows,
a baby now a boy,
a face full of joy.

So young yet so wise
I've been forced to grow
but my bright eyed friend
will love me to the end.

I watch as he plays
in his own little world
His presence here, my fate
my precious little mate.

Shelley Brown

A MIRACLE

I've seen a miracle
On a cold December day
A miracle
I heard a cry
A cry for the joy of life
The miracle of birth and love at first sight.

I've seen a miracle
Left speechless by beauty
A miracle
Words can't express
Can't say what I've seen
A miracle, an angel, a dream.

It's a miracle
For all the world to see
A miracle
Your life's a miracle to me.

R Sims

MIDDLE AGE

Once, we sat quietly at the edge of the little field
Stuck onto the curve of the world;
We watched the sky, bleeding from a wound low on the horizon
Grow Dark;
We drank the wine and talked and said we had too little time
And as the loveliness of the place and the pleasure of being together
Filled us with happiness
A small chill came as a shadow over our world and I cried
You, perhaps, cried inside - I don't know.

Sally Williams

TIME GOES ON

Time goes on
Relentless as the sea,
Flowing on incessantly.
We spend our youth to plan and scheme,
Work so hard to fulfil a dream.
Our chances come and then are gone,
Time goes on.

Time goes on
Fast or slow, time will go,
None of us can halt the flow.
We bear our children, watch them grow
And teach them all they ought to know,
They soon grow up and then are gone,
Time goes on.

Time goes on
Onward through the years,
Through the sunshine, through the tears.
Life cycle gone at rapid rate
And we have passed our sell by date.
Look back on life, where has it gone
Time goes on.

Time goes on
Beyond the crystal sea,
Take us to eternity.
If we accept our God before
He will be waiting on that shore
To take us home, where he has gone
And time goes on and on and on . . .

Berly R Daintree

WHEN APRIL COMES AGAIN

Wood-smoke to heaven like a prayer ascending,
A narrow path, its well-worn way still wending
Beside the stream, beneath the willows bending
Before the April breeze.

Wood-smoke that beckons but there's no returning
Along that path, though lured by memories, yearning
To feel again bright warmth; for love's bright burning
Was quenched in April tears.

And springtime's gone and summer's flowers fast fading,
Ripe autumn fruits from laden boughs cascading
While swallows wait, blue-black and red, parading
Like soldiers lined for war.

Bright leaves begin to fall, wind-whipped, gyrating
Like maddened moths around a flame, and waiting
Grim faced, black-browed, his reign anticipating,
Stands winter at the door.

Though harsh his rule, his frosty heart unfeeling
For blackened rose or ruffled robin reeling
Against his gales, yet faith has its revealing
When April comes again.

Kathleen Law

DELIVERANCE

Suspended, cocooned - in a warm water bed
on full life support, intravenously fed
The months have passed slowly, the end is now near
I must say goodbye to this life I hold dear

I had a twin brother, but since he passed on
I find all the fight that was in me has gone
If blissful hereafter there'd proven to be
he'd promised he'd find a way back to fetch me

I hear muted voices, persuasively calling
and into the blackness I feel myself falling
Forced - squirming - pulled down a slippery funnel . . .
towards a bright light at the end of a tunnel

I've entered an new world - perhaps it's a dream
I'm gasping for air now, I kick and I scream
The voices grow louder - one's thick choked with joy:
'Here, darling - a *sister* for our baby boy!'

Sue Millward

THE LAST CARESS

Bright was the moonlight in the dark velvet sky,
Stars twinkled and shone like diamonds way up high.
Fingers entwined the two walked hand in hand,
The only two lovers in all the land.
They pause by the wide trunk of a chestnut tree,
He gently removes pins to let her hair fall free.
Cupping her face between his large gentle hands,
He kissed her eyes, her nose, with one special brand.
She looks at him with her dark brown eyes,
Like a magician with the power to mesmerise.
Walking once more they approach the big house,
Specially arranged for her and her spouse.
They enter the house with sorrow in their heart,
For her beloved has come the time to depart.
He lies in his bed so peaceful and calm,
His beloved face so beautiful, so pale and so wan.
Over fifty years they had lived and loved,
He holds her hand, saying 'Don't grieve beloved'
Gently she kisses his cold still lips,
His last caress gives in beautiful bliss.
Sometimes he comes to the chestnut tree,
Waiting for the day when she will be free.

Eve Clucas

MIRROR

I look in the mirror
And what do I see?
I see a stranger
Looking at me

I see silver
Where once there was gold
A warning sign
You're getting old

I see the eyes
So dull and grey
No longer blue
Sparkling and gay

I see the wrinkles
The laughter lines too
Where once there was one chin
Now there are two

I see the mouth
Set firm in its way
No longer the smile
That could light up a day

I see a face
That through the years
Has laughed the laughs
And cried the tears

I see an expression
That has known all the pain
Risen above it
And loved again

That face in the mirror
can it really be mine?
Showing the sadness
of the passage of time.

Ann Packman

GOODBYE TO A SPECIAL PERSON
(My Mum)

To my darling mum
I feel so sad without you,
My heart feels broken in two,
I thought you would always be here
When you said 'You felt poorly' we said 'You'll be alright'
You were in pain and had such a lot to bear I know that now,
You loved me so much sometimes I did not show it back,
People say the pain gets easier be strong.
Look at your family you have them they depend on you.
I know all these things are true,
But the pain and sadness I feel is really unbearable
It's not easy being able to share things with you.
We go to your grave and put flowers there,
I talk to you and Anita as you are there together
Just to say I love you and be able to put my arms around you
I never thought I would lose you as 63 years old is still young
Spring is here your favourite time of the year.
I want you to rest in heaven,
I hope it's a lovely place where you meet old friends,
Words cannot express how I love you and miss you.
Take care my darling
I will try to be strong
I love you 'Mum'
Goodbye for now.

L E Schoepp

PASSED AWAY

I spoke to you what only seemed like only yesterday,
Heard from a close friend that you had passed away,
Alone, in a hospital ward you died peacefully in your sleep,
Attended your funeral, watched the mourners weep,
The rain lashed down relentlessly on our bowed heads,
As the minister gave the last rites to the dead,
With a lifeless stare I watched them lower your coffin into the ground,
Looked up through the black clouds and hoped that heaven you had found,
The service ended, we all quietly left the unhappy scene,
Left with only memories of what you had been.

Graeme Muir

HONESTY

My glass shall not persuade me I am old.
I look and then forget what I did see.
Where e'er I go I bring myself quite bold,
Say what is there was given to me free.
The smile that makes the creases in my face,
The head that has a mind which now and then
Forgets what times have passed without a trace
Except for dates and facts inscribed by pen.
I know that now the years are passing by,
No space to put the candles on the cake.
The stairs I climb remind me now my bones
Are creaking carefully with gentle ache.
But still I know that days, early or late,
In spite of winds and fog, when weather cold,
Skies are blue and so convince me to state
My glass shall not persuade me I am old.

Sister Gregory Feetenby

SENIOR CITIZENS 1996

I have friends who think the same as me,
We ask, why are we here when health fails to be
good and strong, no aches and pains for us,
Instead the niggles, they cause depressions fuss.

Gone are the days when we used to rush about,
Get excited and noisy and sing and shout,
Getting old was years away without a doubt,
All to soon we're aged and grey, and grouch.

We are advised to make the most of the days,
No second chance, rehearsals are for plays,
Trips to clubs and outings, and I must say,
What would we do without them, fade away.

Money really helps if you can't move too well,
Pays for taxi trips if you happen to be frail,
We hate to be a problem to our families it's clear,
Try to be as happy as we can, never fear.

Once a week we have pension day, a big event,
Meet friends for a chat, then sort out the rent,
Put money away for bills, council tax, and such,
What's left for food and clothes, not much.

The charity shops do a trade for different clothes,
High fashion not needed for us I suppose,
On the whole our requirements are met,
We can be happy with the bargains we get.

We all know getting old is a worrying time,
The ups and downs costing more than a dime,
But when the weather is bleak and it's a miserable day,
It's bliss to lie in, take breakfast on a tray.

Vi Talman

WE COME, WE GO

Into this world
We noisily come,
First signs of abuse
A slap on the bum,
Then mum gives a cuddle
To stop all the crying,
Then come the visitors
Wide-eyed and prying.
Then all too soon
School days are here,
She leaves us there
In her eye there's a tear.
We just cant wait
For our teenage years
When we face the unexpected
The joys and the fears.
Adult years bring reality,
Decisions, worries and pain,
Our parents warned us often enough,
Now the cycle starts over again.
And when our days are numbered
And the master calls us home
We leave this world with nothing
The same way that we come.

Gladys McFall

YOUR WEDDING DAY

Waking up with a throbbing head,
wishing it was the day before instead.
Your wedding day has arrived at last,
your wild days of freedom have now past.
The night before fades quickly from your mind
Soon the register you will have signed.

Your dress is hanging from a hook on the wall,
layers of satin and lace seem to call.
In a few more minutes the silence will break
Oh how you wish you could banish this headache!
Your body begins to tingle, you can't sit still
and you can't help but feel excitedly ill.

A smile grows upon your face
your heart is beating a hurried pace.
You roll up the bedroom blind,
to see that the weather is being kind
From downstairs you can hear some chatter,
your mother and sister having a natter.

The time has come for you to take hold of the day,
the excitement of it all causes you to sway.
Your mother brings you up a hearty meal,
to try and place you on an even keel.
The clock is ticking away the time for you,
it will soon be your chance to say 'I do'

Cindy Teague

EARTH CYCLE

At the beginning of time so beautiful
Covered in flowers, trees and grass
A paradise for both man and beast
Things have changed for the worse - alas

Now her forests are hacked down
Her crystal, sparkling waters polluted
Her minerals and precious stones
By mankind have been looted

Ravaged and mistreated by the human race
No longer stable or predictable these days
The protection and nourishment we took for granted from birth,
Cannot be sustained forever from our mother - Planet Earth.

Elizabeth Amery

A TIME SO FARAWAY

A soft feather bed with a soft feather quilt,
So high off the ground for a giant it seemed built
Where I, as a child, did dreams all my dreams
But how faraway from me now it all seems.

Did I ever climb those narrow stairs
And kneel by that bed and there say my prayers?
Thanking the Lord, for each day done,
God bless Dad, God bless Mum.

And waiting for me on the very top stair
A scruffy old, loved-to-bits, worn Teddy Bear
That every child holds while dreaming its dreams
But how faraway from me now it all seems.

Barbara MacDonald

SUMMER TO WINTER

(Inspired by Sister Mercy)

When you are a child the days are long
And summer goes on forever
But when your children start to arrive
The days are short and the nights are long
Broken with their cries
When they grow and all leave home
The days go flashing by
The summers do not seem as long
As in the good old days gone by
But still the nights can be long
As in your bed you lie
Wondering and worrying are they alright
If only they would ring me
And say 'Yes mum I am OK'
But maybe I expect too much
They have their own lives to lead
But I wish that they would stop and think
One day they will get old
But when you are young and enjoying life
And summer goes on forever
You do not stop to think
About life's winter weather
Maybe I am just getting old
And summer cannot last forever
But I still have your love
To share our winter together.

Joan Fowler

THE ROUTINES OF LIFE

Why am I here?
Does this life have a purpose,
a meaning
or is it just a matter of routine
Is there some hidden purpose
of which I am not aware
but one that is known by someone
surely someone somewhere is bound to know
why I am here.

Must I live my life as a matter of routine?
Must I live and breathe in an internal dimension
where there is neither beginning nor end
co-existing with the elements, with nature
someone somewhere must know why I am here.

There must be a reason for this routine
that is called life
someone knows but is unwilling to share that knowledge
until it is too late
so I am left wondering, always wondering
why I am here
forming a part of the circle, the pattern
that is called life
that is called routine.

Charles MacIntyre

A PART OF LIFE

I wonder where he is
I wonder what he's doing

where he has been
who has he seen

90

what's happening to me
I don't understand

I think I have just fallen in love

Jane Brady

MY DAUGHTERS

Yes my daughters three I've got
and to me are worth a lot
they are all of different ages
Because my life as been in stages
My oldest one herself a mother
and swears that she won't have another
I used to be just like you
But then came baby number two
the second one is in her teens
and doesn't know just what life means
at that age we are all the same
looking for someone else to blame
and at last there is my youngest
She brings love and joy among us
I've told you now about all three
and just how much they mean to me
I love them all so very dear
and for their safety I sometimes fear
I wish to be with them for ever
But I know that I could never
One day when they have all left home
then I will feel just so alone
So this I dedicate to them
and hope that they'll remember when
days when we were all together
could I forget 'No not ever'

Elaine Jenkins

SAILING A SWINGBOAT

Up and forward,
Back and down,
At the fairground
Thrills abound.
Attractions, music,
Laughter and screams,
Blend in the heart
To rekindle old dreams.
The styles and opinions
Of a different age,
Tread yet again
The nostalgic stage.
Speeding and swerving,
Hold on tight!
Bumping and bouncing,
Heads feel light.
The flashing of colours,
The dazzling of eyes,
Congratulations,
You've just won a prize.
Ice-cream and candy floss,
Popcorn and sweets,
Hot chips and lemonade,
A feastful of treats.
And the lads and the lassies
Exchange those glances,
That lead to a kiss
And new romances.
And as their happy evening fades
And home the revellers go,
Another summer will burn away
And older they must grow.

Paul Hutton

THE CIRCLE OF LIFE

There is that just once in a lifetime,
It could be the day you were born
Into a happy, loving family is a sign,
A new world is beginning at dawn.

From a toddler to a teenager is quite exciting
For some its fun but some, it could be frightening.
We search for the silver lining always
And always counting on our lucky days.

Then one day, the dreams come true,
Happiness is longed for, especially for you,
Wedding bells are ringing,
With sounds of angels singing.

Everything in life looks rosy and blooming,
Living in a garden of Eden is assuming
A wonderful life is everyone's desire,
Remembering there is no smoke without fire.

Then a child is expected,
Perfection in every way, like a dream is selected,
Sometimes that dream comes true
And nothing could be the same, if only we knew.

As they grow up before your very eyes,
How much happiness and sorrows we accept with sighs,
But then it was all worthwhile,
Because with love and pride, they take that step up the aisle.

And now the continuation of love carries on,
Even though our life has almost gone.
We are looking forward to that silver lining,
Like stars in the sky, our love will always be shining.

Beryl Sylvia Rusmanis

A PROUD MOTHER

Is it a boy?
Is it a girl?
The pain and the worry
and finally the glory
of knowing your child.
A bundle of blankets
are piled, on top and around
your child.
Tender love, tender care, and
another mouth to feed.
Mother and Father are
Proud and pleased,
money to spend on someone else.
Is it a girl?
Is it a boy?

Amelia Mankelow

PEACE PERFECT PEACE

If we could wake up one morning and find all the world at peace.
No more fighting and sorrow, no more anger and grief.
God made the world to live in with beautiful colours to see
A place for us to be happy, peace for you and me
I think of all the people who are far worse off than me.
The sick the wounded, the handicapped, and those who cannot see,
I feel I ought to be happy, contented and glad
If only there was peace, instead of feeling sad.
So if we want to be happy, we must think of the good things in life
Forget all the fighting and bitterness the anger and strife.
Perhaps one day we will find that peace we all have been waiting for.
To share with our loved ones whom we adore.

Olive Peck

ONLY ONCE

Through this life
We come but once;
Savour all you can
And more.
Enjoy the life
And health therein;
No more
You'll come this way.

Watch the youths
Who used to be;
Ageing fast
In front of you.
Travelling down
Yes, the same road
Only once
For them as well.

Silver threads
Mixed in with gold;
Peach like skin of youth
Begins to crumble.
Wrinkles
Now appear;
The signs of what
Is happening
Are there
For you to see.

Catherine O'Kane

MOVING ON AND ON

I was born in the West Midlands
And grew up when the war was on
When I got married
To Shropshire I moved on
Then because of circumstances
To Northern Ireland I had gone
It is hard to describe
The sense of peace I felt
I've now lived here for 30 years
The peace has come and gone
In a small village I live
I have no desire to go back
The feeling is of content
Which other places lack
The neighbours are the best
And I do not relent
Because Northern Ireland is nicer than the rest
Things can only get better
Or so they say
And life goes on and on
Along its own merry way.

Joyce Evans

MORNING AFTER MOODS AT SCHOOL

On one of the few nights a year, the teachers
And pupils enjoyed a rapport schooldays rarely
Attained. Lesson time tempers were common features
Unfortunately; blame was dealt out unfairly
To children who showed they were still merry creatures,
Upholding last evening's mood debonairly.
Perhaps, blustering nights, with hail in the rain spoil
Thoughts of the best outing for weeks; plus the toil

Involved in creating a memorable show
For parents arriving, right then, in the car-park.
Perhaps they prefer to recall a fiasco,
Denying the magic - the éclat - the brave spark
Rehearsal work generated, half a term ago.
Order returns. Teachers find papers to mark,
And post-mortems on tests set last Friday.
Their last word is, 'Please, people, *Leave This Room Tidy*!'

Gillian Fisher

PLAIN SAILING

Nothing touches the beautiful ship.
In full sail she appears
To be happily sweeping blue seas,
Specks of white foam frothing,
The ship is on an even keel,
The lifeboat on board will
Never be needed. No fear
Of collision, being washed
Overboard. Never meeting
Trials or tribulations, dreaded
Storms or squalls. No
Buffeting about - a serene
And placid existence,
Uneventful, with nothing to disturb
The inner peace and tranquillity,
That the ship bestows on to
The outside world. Cushioned,
Guarded and cocooned, sheltered
And treasured - Plain Sailing
Always, for a beautiful ship in a
Plain glass bottle.

Betty Eileen Houghland

A NEW BEGINNING

Ripped from my tedious job
by an urgent phone call,
I drive through the wet streets
thick with cars and red traffic signals.

The hospital is awash
with alien smells
and unmitigated blue walls
that rush past ad infinitum.

Thrust out from the pain,
a proud new life
screams
it's fragile
exultation;
my daughter is born.

Benjamin F Jones

CHILDHOOD TRAVELS

I remember when quite small
Being blindfolded in the hall,
Going on an exciting flight
Higher and higher in the night.

In my mind I could see
I was right over the cherry tree,
And I heard my uncle's words
'Please be careful of the birds.'

To earth with a bump I came down.
Off with the blindfold, on with a frown,
Because blinded by the light after the gloom,
I realised I was in our sitting room.

Joan G Brown

CHILDREN

Children are given to us with love,
To borrow for just a short time,
Until the day comes for them to leave-
Is just a short reprieve.
Love them as you only know how;
Let them see how much you care.
Children expect love as their fate,
Remember- tomorrow is too late!

Valerie Marshall

CIRCLE OF LIFE

Yesterday was once today
today will soon be yesterday
tomorrow will be today.

The present will become the past,
the future will be the present,
and an unknown time will be the future.

The circle goes on, it never ends,
because a circle has no end,
like a wheel, the wheel of life.

We join the wheel, others leave,
we are born, we grow, we live,
we know joys and sorrows, tears and happiness

Love and loneliness, marriage and death,
yesterday perhaps we were sad,
today happy, tomorrow is unknown.

The circle goes on, forever turning, turning . . .

Marge Chamberlain

MY TWIN SISTER

I've got a twin sister, she looks just like me
When we're together we're as happy as can be
We started school and we sat together
We'd swap our seats to confuse the teacher
Our exam marks were close as a rule
They stayed much the same right through school
We studied, we laughed, and played together
This was how it would be for ever
We had lots of friends who were lots of fun
Holidays with the family in the sun
We were taught piano and played duets
And kept a dog and rabbits as pets
We took up typing and shorthand too
So when we left school we'd have something to do
On leaving school we learned about weeds
We got jobs together at Sutton Seeds
We learned about fruits, roses and plants
Our knowledge of gardening this job did enhance
We typed letters to places far and near
Our bosses were nice, we loved it here
A boy from the warehouse was our best friend
He settled for me in the end
We moved to a cottage just round the corner
So's I could be near my twin sister
She too fell in love and on her wedding day
Moved to a cottage fifty miles away
Though we're now this distance apart
She's always with me in my heart.

Mary Loader

FOOTPRINTS

A man and an angel stood talking
They looked at each other and started walking
The man said there are still many things I don't understand
The angel replied let's look at your footprints in the sand
When you were young and very strong
You stepped out and your stride was long
Shoulders back so very proud
Standing out in any crowd
Your life never falters not even a pause
Now there are new prints next to yours
This is the happiest time of your life
For those new prints belong to your wife
Dancing along every step is a skip
Never a tumble or even a trip
Until one day
I am afraid to say
As you walk hand in hand
Two prints now drag in the sand
As they wander from side to side
You are trying to be their guide
Doing your best to keep them straight
Straining from carrying the extra weight
One set of prints disappear one day
This is when your wife passed away
The man snapped where were you when I needed you most of all
The angel replied I was there ready for your fall
With a broken heart you had given up too
The lone steps were mine I was carrying you.

P E Cox

TIMES OF LIFE

Each age has its compensations
Advantages and inspirations
Tragedies and complications
Hopes for our tomorrows

When we are young we rush around
Up on the swing down on the ground
Laughing and giggling up the trees
Falling and crying with damaged knees

Teen ages should be happy years
First there's joy then there's tears
We really think we'll go insane
We fall in love then out again

Middle age brings toil and work
Not a moment left to shirk
Elderly parents need our care
Grandchildren bring us joys to share

Old age gives us time to dwell
Upon the days of yore
To sit and relate stories and really be a bore
And get away with many things we never could before.

Every age has its jubilations
Roads that lead to destinations
Ups and downs and confrontations
Happiness and sorrows.

Ethel M Hatfield

TEA IN THE HALLS

Tea in the halls,
Embarrassed silence as parents hovered.
I look for acceptance in the gathering
of anonymous faces.
The jingling of tea cups and rambling chatter
upset the unease.
'All the best Sean, We'll go on now'
I feel released from the burden of their expectations.
As they leave I inch forward searching for a
welcoming smile.
Wondering why I feel so very very alone.

Sean Anderson

LIFE

The world goes on living year after year
but there is no-one to tell us why we are here
Why do we live if only to die
where's the almighty to tell us why
If God does exist and man his invention
why does he not speak and answer our questions?
Why do we love if only to lose?
Why is there disaster all over the news?
Why do we fight in a bloody war?
And kill fellow man, what is it for?
Why does a young baby die in his sleep?
Why was that life given if not to keep?
We live our lives and do what we do
just passing the time until time is through
Why are we happy if only to be sad?
Why is all the good followed by bad?
There is sadness and sorrow, things to make us cry
When will somebody show to tell us why? . . .

Ian Seal

FULL CIRCLE

The sun that shines
and the moon's soft glow.
Centuries pass, all is the same.
Gently the waves lap the shore,
all goes on just like before.

Trees who shed their autumn leaves
upon the earth's soft core.
Beauty of flowers that grow and bloom,
and rivers onward ever flow.
Rain and frost, ice and snow.

Flashing lightning, thunder roars,
stormy seas, tempests blow,
colours of rainbows, waterfalls,
twinkling stars and mountains tall.

Seasons come, seasons go,
repeatedly day turns to night,
we are born, we die
but time goes by.
Full circle to the end of time.

Gladys Bree

PEACE

In the moment before death
comes the silence of darkness
The rise and fall of one last breath.
No more the sound of a heartbeat
At last peace within yourself,
For death you cannot cheat.
Now as all emotions wane
In the final act of life,
You will feel no pain.

T Read

DECISION

To everyone during life's span
          There's a time to debate
A time for decision to be made
          Before it's too late.

In that hour of need
          Only one decree to heed
To exclude all others
          Right or wrong
When the time for debating
          Has come and gone.

When every minute of every hour
          Seems like an eternity
A conflict will ensue
          To find the one to chose
Win or lose
          A final policy to pursue

Like the wish from a coin in a fountain
          Only one will be blessed
The final decision chosen from all the rest

There's wisdom in that one decision
          Or plan
For some things we cannot change
          Courage to make a choice
To change the things we can

To abide by that decision
          To chance a throw with that dice of life
Is the hallmark
          Of the facts of life.

Samuel Victor Smy

DIVORCE?

I'm not very happy to see my dad go
Mum and dad aren't together
She runs her own show
Why did they split up
Nobody knows
They say not to worry, but whose
taking the blows.

Love went through the window,
It went, somewhere else
Now it is quiet, it's not the same house
No more family dinners, no more
good times to be had
Maybe they're happy, but it's
driving me mad.

Who shall I stick with, my
mum or my dad
It's not very easy, it's making me sad.
Let's just stick together, try
and be a family once more.
I haven't been the same
since my dad walked out
the door.

Carl Prosser

TO ETERNITY

Grieve not at death
For all the pain you feel
Is proof that life was good,
And love was real;
Let go your grief,
And one day you will see
That love endures
For all eternity.

As long as you can remember me
I shall not die,
Recall me please with laughter
Not a sigh,
Though death may claim me
Love is stronger,
And safe within your heart
I love thee longer.

Frances Fry

TO BEEF OR NOT TO BEEF?

Don't eat beef, for BSE
Will get you in the end
Burgers, steaks and sausages
All send you mad my friend.

Eggs causing salmonella
And chickens too maybe
Then additives in food and drinks
Plus caffeine in our tea.

Too much salt is dangerous
And please cut off all fat
Then there's hydrogenisation
But we won't go into that!

They're warning now of pesticides
On fruit and veg and stuff
For it's becoming lethal
But if you die - that's tough!

Don't worry. here's my solution,
Tell me quick - you call
We'll boycott all the lot I say
And just don't eat at all!

Elaine Seagrave

THE CIRCLE OF LIFE

It's hard being stuck in the middle
Neither young nor old,
No excuse for not knowing
Nearly too old to be told

It takes a long time to look lovely,
And nearly as long to look fine
Never again to look youthful
Too young not to mind.

Your children are still your children
Even when they've grown bigger than you
Now they sit still at your table
Make conversation that you used to do.

Your look at your life and wonder
What fate has in store for you
And remembering the past you shudder
Hoping the future will do.

The best thing to do is look forward
And forget what went before
It's the only way to get through it
To accept it and come back for more.

Pauline Davison

FINAL DESTINATION

There is room somewhere
Into which we all will step
There is plenty of space there
For everyone who goes inside

The light is bright and warm
A welcome is assured
We are protected from harm
And greeted with arms open wide

We are home at last in that place
We can rest and understand
Without life's burdens and pace
Time is gone, we are on the other side

The final destination, our goal
This room we enter in love
The room prepared for our soul
Where love lives - it never died.

June Kasaven

REFLECTIONS

I sit and watch him with a sideward glance.
He who once made my heart dance

Winter snow lies on his aged peak
and craggy rocks his face beneath.

We shared a life, we shared a home
We loved our children
but now they're gone

What do you think?
Are you aware of feeling, sadness
                                    and despair.

I want to shout and cry and yell
We can escape this dreary hell

Alas, we stay, we suffer on.
We don't look back, we don't look on
towards a nicer happier time
When we were lovers and
lived as one.

Olwen Brooks

TIME

Time stands still for no man.
Pleasure turns to pain.
April brings the showers.
May dries up the rain.

Roses bloom in June's warm haze,
Holidays in July.
August time for harvest
September swallows fly.

Tick the days that pass so quick,
Right before our eyes.
Savour every minute.
Make the most of our short lives.

Rebecca Howells

A GALE BLOWS - SONNET

A gale blows all around me, but tranquil
Is the storm: a beak sweet dipped in twilight,
Sings night away from morn. Dulcet tones trill
Moving notes, and from my eyes rush a rill.
Blow male nightingale, your gale in the night,
Your song does burnish a lustreless sky,
And finds the misty orbit of my eye.
I weigh weightless tunes way above in space,
As shackled tears I cry freedom 'neath my face.
Evensong dies with a pure melody,
My hands clasp in prayer so naturally,
I see heaven and earth in harmony:
An old song has flown a new one now wings,
A gale blows again, a nightingale sings.

William Edward Lewis (Jnr)

YESTERDAY

It seems like only yesterday when I was young and free.
I had no cares nor worries, the world belonged to me.
Each day was like a miracle, a fantasy of dreams,
With all my loved ones round me, only yesterday it seems.

My granddad held my hands so tight, as across the fields we'd trek.
To pick bluebells and primroses, by teatime we'd be back.
He taught me to make a daisy chain and placed it in my hair,
He said I was his Princess and I wished he'd always be there.

My granny meant the world to me, she was so kind and good.
When she took me on her knee, she taught me all she could.
She said one time I'll ne'er forget, I seem to hear her still,
'Remain a child as long as you can, you've a lifetime to fulfil'.

My Granddad he is gone now, my granny's old and grey.
And I myself have changed now from that child of yesterday.
But Oh! How I remember when I was free and wild,
I wish I could bring back those days when I was just
A child.

Tanya Fisher

DIVISION

We met
We multiplied
Subtracted the nasty bits
                (like accumulating debts)
Added unnecessary luxuries
                (like a second car)
Then . . .
We divided it

Kathleen Bradley

JOURNEY'S END

Is there a road without a bend
Which I can travel to my journey's end
For some the road is long and narrow
For others I fear a lonely furrow,
The rules of life must hold sway
For those who travel the life's highway,
To judge and be judged is how we must live
Instead of taking we must give,
To face the world with a cheerful smile
For the road we travel can be many a mile,
There is a road without a bend
For me to travel to my journey's end.

Jack Carver

AND FINALLY

I stare bewildered from my 'cot',
strange faces peer down at me,
A nurse approaches, smiling . . . bath-time!
Clean once more: new nappy fitted
Smelling of roses
More voices approach
hustle, bustle
I lay,
I can't communicate
Saliva dribbles from my mouth
It's wiped away efficiently.
Whispers above me
talking about me
'She's only got a few hours left'
People talk about me, not to me.
treated like a new-born infant
So I began, so shall I end . . .

Kate Jackson

THE CIRCLE OF LIFE

Little baby sweet and new
What has fate mapped out for you?
As you lay gurgling in your pram
I pray you'll grow up free from harm.

In a few years time you will be off to school
And learn to swim in the local pool,
Settling down to read and write
With studies and homework to do at night.

The troublesome teens you will have to get through
Friends and relationships could make you feel blue!
Try to get by with a smile on your face
As you grow demurely, full of grace.

Then there will be the occasion of your marriage
Looking so beautiful, as you travel in horse and carriage,
A handsome groom lovingly by your side
A compliment to the gorgeous bride.

Children one day you will have of your own
A welcome blessing to add to your home,
You will watch them grow in your tender care
With hardly a moment for you to spare.

The circle of life will continue around
Then one day you will have found
That life goes on around you come what may
I pray good health, and happiness will come to stay.

Life is the greatest gift God gave
Walk in his footsteps and try to be brave,
Meet your troubles in life head on
And feel satisfaction for a job well done.

Lorna Culshaw

THE CIRCLE OF LIFE

It only seems like yesterday
when I was a child.

The excitement of simple things,
like going to the fair.
Please, please can I have a
toffee apple, tugging at my
mother's sleeve.

Then came the teenage years,
Blushing whenever anybody
looked at you, soon took over
the ability to flirt.

Marriage came, this is for
life so we were told.
Children followed, oh the delight.
It wasn't long before I was
seeing them through their
awkward years.

My marriage is now over
I look in the mirror, the
lines have appeared, after
going through a tunnel
the light has emerged.

We all have to learn
the lessons of life, and
each experience takes us
nearer our goal.

I am now looking forward
to what years I have left,
and with the love of
my children I am the
fortunate one.

Pauline Jackson

PRECIOUS TIMES

You brought such joy when you appeared
And a love I've never known
I've watched you through the many years
As into adulthood you've grown

A parent's work is hard to do
There are no definite rules
It's difficult to guide you straight
When hampered by many fools

I'm not the best Mum in the world
But I've always done my best
And the trials of life have certainly
Put me to the test

You've been my inspiration
To get up when I've been down
You've made me laugh, instead of cry
And made me smile, not frown

Life is so strange in many ways
It's a tangled web we weave
You've relied on me all those years
Then you up and leave

I look back through the many years
And how the time has flown
For now, my son, you have a son
Of your very own

Give him the love, that I gave you
As the circle of life goes by
And make the most of these precious years
'Cos, believe me, they do fly.

Jill Thompson

THE CIRCLE OF LIFE

We are conceived and born
Without a by your leave
So we start living our lives
Trying hard to please.

Then we go to school
Without a by your leave
To learn our lessons
Trying hard to please.

We leave, get a job
Without a by your leave
To earn a living
Trying hard to please.

We get married
Without a by your leave
Produce children
Trying hard to please.

Then we die; go to heaven
Without a by your leave
God asks 'What have you
Done with your life?'
I tried hard to please.

Wilf Hall

TO STELLA

When you were very young, and I a sage.
When I could guide you through each living stage.
Then was life good to me in every sense,
And I received your love; sweet recompense.

Now time has passed and you are wiser far.
You're teaching me what real values are.
Cycle of life completed in its move,
And I repay you ever with my love.

Knutsson

THEY THINK MOTHER'S 'PAST IT'

Oh Mother, you're stupid and getting so fat.
When I get to your age I won't look like *that!*
Oh mother, are you blind? Can't you thread your own needle?
Remember your glasses and don't be so feeble.

Oh Mother, are you deaf, can't you answer the 'phone?
If it's Tom or Dick just say I'm not home.
Oh Mother, your memory's going too I see.
That's four times today you've lost the car key.

Oh Mother, you're untidy, you must waste all day.
They think I do nothing to earn full time pay!
Oh Mother, don't sing, your tune is all wrong.
Your teeth are decayed and it's spoiling the song.

Oh Mother, my driving test is next week.
You can sit in your car but don't dare to speak.
Oh Mother, last concert duet's not forgotten.
She was alright but Mum was rotten.

So Mother if you ever perform again.
You must first write a poem to prove you are sane.
So dear Mother is now on her final test.
Whose side are you on - mine, or the *rest*?

Deborah Meanley

MAYBE I'M AMAZED

I thank you God, my heavenly Father,
That you have been with me
Through these days of toil and grief,
Of upward journey.
You are the same yesterday today and forever.

You were with me when I was a little baby,
A growing lad, a rebellious teenager,
And an older softer gentleman.

You will be with me for all eternity,
Giving encouragement, sometimes correction,
And often a much needed kick up the backside!

God will be with me on my onward journey.
To where, to what, to whom,
You only know.

He will encompass me with blessing,
As water laps against the seashore.

Thank you that you will be with me,
In the difficult times as well as the joys,
The pains, the sorrows,
Through thick and thin.

Your love reaching out,
Giving strength, supporting others.
Thank you.

Maybe I am just amazed
At the way you really love me.

Christopher J Symonds

CHANGE

The candle of life is burning away,
What was once the future is now today,
Where there was time there is no time at all,
Where there once was an open road,
There now stands a wall.

As the candle burns down
To the flicker of a flame,
There is no sound,
There is no pain,
A whiff of smoke rises
As the flame finally dies.

At that very moment,
The completion of the circle,
Somewhere a new born baby cries,
And another journey begins.

T S Norman

REFLECTIONS

When I look in the mirror, what do I see?
A sad lonely woman staring back at me.
Her lips can recall a thousand promises
That her ears have been told
And her eyes reflect the pain and misery
In her life as she grows old.
She smiles to herself as she remembers a dream,
That life used to be so perfect, or so it seemed.
She then sheds a tear that falls down her face
As she realises she's outlived this awful place,
She turns her head and faces away,
Back to reality and leaves the reflections at bay.

Cindy Ellis

REGENERATION

So time has cut his harvest prematurely?
A week, a day will pass and then no matter -
The land is ploughed, the stems are tied securely.
Experience is wind and he can scatter
Reapers and worried labourers like chaff.
Who guards the empty acres under frost?
Who makes the scarecrow sign his epitaph?
Who is it eats the grain? Who counts the cost?
Never the lovers bending in the corn
Wondering when to cut and watching rain;
Never the child of summer lately born
Gazing in azure distances, the plain
Of idle grasses murmuring like rhyme
And sighing to themselves, 'There is no time .'

Alasdair Aston

NOW THAT THE FIGHTING HAS STOPPED

Masses of bodies just lying around
After the fighting had stopped
Masses of poppies covering the ground
When from the planes they were dropped.

Bullet cases, empty shells
Unexploded bombs.
Crying people, lonely bells.
White crosses on the tombs.

Back to the homes we once adored
Food in the stores where we once shopped
Friendship and loving at last restored
Now that the fighting has stopped!

Richard Griffiths (13)

AFRAID OF THE DARK?

I was afraid of the dark;
I remember times as a child
peering over the edge of blankets
in a bed that in the dark seemed vast.
Wondering if tonight at last
the monstrous bogeyman would appear.
I recall how I'd lie
motionless with fear,
Believing if I moved I'd die,
And how my heart was thudding so hard
I would clasp my hands over my chest
so that 'it' in the corner wouldn't hear
and tear the offending noise from my breast.

Even now that I'm grown
there are times in the dark
when I think of the bogeyman,
And I wonder, what if? As just for a lark.
a foot comes from under the duvet,
Is slowly lowered to the floor,
And I dare the abomination, that terrible grey
horror lurking under my bed, to claw
at my flesh with its talons.
Just because I've not yet succeeded
in waiting to see what happens
doesn't mean my actions are impeded
by a long ago fear of the dark.

Alexander K Stubbs

MY GREAT ADVENTURE . . .

I wrestled barehanded with a lion,
With huge gleaming emerald eyes!
. . . Was marooned on a tropical island,
Blitzed by blue buzzing flies.

I bit back a shark that attacked me,
It prized great gaping jaws and big teeth;
An octopus trailing tentacles fifty feet long -
Dragged me over a coral reef.

Blinking: I still faced the lion,
On bedside cabinet cutely displayed . . .
A mosquito hovered somewhere in the room -
The toy, jaws was on the wardrobe arrayed.

My feline friend had playfully scrammed my leg,
Ruckled my sheet was my giant octopus . . .
My great adventure was merely a dream -
No need to fret or fuss.

True life escapades are all very fine,
But if nobody minds . . . I'll just dream mine.

Christina Angelique

ETERNAL WATER

I watch him swim,
One arm in front of the other,
Head pushing back through the crystal
clear water.
His feet flapping
Face in and out of the water
He swims with such speed and grace
Creating in me such inspiration.
He swims and swims

Yet has no destination.
His body undulating up and down,
He creates such a perfect pattern
Like a circle going round and round.

Roshida Begum

SANTA

I awoke quite early one Christmas morning
and saw something bright at the foot of my bed.
There was someone there, no, I wasn't dreaming.
Why it was good old Santa Claus, all dressed in red.
I lay quite still, heart thumping, my eyes shut tight,
for fear he'd vanish if I gave him a fright.

It seemed ages and ages that I lay there
hardly daring to breathe, but wanting to peek,
For to actually see him was very rare,
friends would be jealous when I told them next week.
At last, I could open my eyes, it was light.
No, Santa wasn't there, but oh, what a sight!

A large rocking horse it had been that I'd seen
for it was bright red all except for its mane.
I climbed out of bed shouting 'He's been, he's been'
and jumped on his back, holding tight to the rein.
It didn't matter I hadn't seen Santa,
as I rocked to and fro, pretending to canter.

Christmases have come and gone, but every year
I think of that time I'd thought Santa was there.
Knowing how lucky I am, full of good cheer,
to have children around with whom I can share,
those happy memories from my own childhood,
and say - He'll come tonight if you're really good!

Sheila Collins

TEMPUS FUGIT

Feet behind, impatient walk
Folk a-rushing, no time to spare.
Madam's trolley clipped my leg
I totter - do they care?

Hustle, bustle - here I am -
Stick in hand - a gammy knee
You'd think they're marching with the band
- I struggle, do they see me?

Just an old man, bag in hand
Mellow are my years
She I lost to 'Another land'
-Forgive me all my tears

I must exist, despite my lonesome,
Creep along at steady pace
Thinking wistfully, how I used to run
-To win the egg and spoon race.

The me inside is young at heart
But age has taken toll,
There's no escape for another start
Do I hear a beckoning knoll?

From womb to cradle - toddler boy
First long trousers - manly shave
Work, then marriage, birth, such joy
As children she me gave.

So in your busy daily life
Spare a thought for folks like me.
Cherish your partner, husband or wife
Time will pass you, as it has me.

Kay House

THE CIRCLE OF LIFE

Round and round in a circle
All life has a gentle flow
We are here to experience and learn
All that we may need to know

There will be many compartments of living
Interchangeable facets of life
The joys indeed the sadness
The positivity and the darker strife

This will be the experience
What indeed we are all here for
To sample the delights of this world
So eventually we can become 'More'

More knowledgeable and more aware
More attuned to the finer things
Then we can flow with 'The Circle of Life'
And see what our destiny brings

Birth, life, death and again re-birth
Is the cycle that nature shows
Why should we be any different
Is there re-incarnation do you suppose?

Many choices are indeed our own
I think we must all remember this
If we want to make our lives worth the living
And finally experience our destination of 'Bliss'

For we are mainly in charge of us
So choose to steer a 'Loving' course
Then 'The Circle of Life' will bring 'Joyous Abundance'
Given Generously from 'The one great source.'

Jade Deacon

THE DIAMOND WEDDING

In their marital bed the old couple wake,
Say a daily 'Thank-you' to God for the fact,
And finding limbs that take a lifetime to stir
Sprint with their minds
to a July morning sixty years ago
when shapely legs stepped into stockings of white,
And a tie circled around a proud neck,
While hands plucked bouquets of joy
from a day which ended in a firework of confetti
that lit up the decades.
Sons, grandsons, great granddaughter and son -
The faces of three generations
eclipse the pain
of friends' names
crossed from the Christmas list.

The couple weld sixty wedded years
with a squeeze of the hand,
Lock eyes, smile and triumphantly say:
'We made it'

Carolyn Cox

MY DAUGHTER'S WEDDING

There's my daughter smiling bright,
Looking lovely dressed in white,
Youthful, blushing as a bride,
As I stand proudly by her side.

Am I losing? Will I gain?
Although I know the family name
Will not continue as I want,
With future Christenings at the Font.

126

I glance towards her choice of spouse,
Who'll take her from me to his house,
A smart and healthy looking man
To help her with life's future plan.

I heard the vicar in a low voice say
Who's giving the Bride away?
My child, I handed to her choice,
As I affirmed with father's voice.

R W Curwen

THE DORMANT PART INSIDE YOU

At the core of your being, deep, deep within you
there is a spark burning bright and true
But its light has been veiled
And you feel you have failed

If only you could see yourself through my eyes you would know
The beauty that is dormant in you, yet struggling to flow
And although you don't believe that you will make it - I know
One day you will, for you are constantly trying to grow

I know it is a long and hard journey - I've been there
But always when I got stuck there were people for me in my despair
Now it is your turn and it is about time too
Until you can love yourself I will be there for you

The light within you is an endless flow of energy
And although it may seem extinct to you I know it can burn free
I will keep on gently nurturing that light until you too can see
The radiance and power of your true beauty.

Olivia Guérin

GERIATRIC

The ward light casts a yellow glow
I watch the shadows fall,
A rasping snore and my heart sinks low
The long night looms ahead.

My thoughts take wing
I'm a girl again in a field of golden corn,
Blue skies above, blue eyes beneath
On the day my love was born.

You took my hand and held me close,
We walked through the golden days,
I saw true love in your blue eyes
The world through a rosy haze.

A shaft of moonlight crosses my bed
Like the satin I wore as a bride.
The flowers I carried are long since dead
Pressed in my book of life.

My book tells all of my sorrows and joys
And the life which together we spent.
You still hold my hand in the gathering gloom
And I wait for your blue eyes to smile.

Daylight breaks, the ward comes to life
Scurrying feet and the banging of doors,
Signs of impatient youth so bright,
Once my feet were as light as yours.

Don't pity me young Florence
As you look on this ageing frame
Lift high your head, look life in the face
And please, please remember my name.

Joan Leedale

LEARNING

As we walk along this path of life so long
And our feelings turn from weak to strong.
No matter what age we find ourselves in time,
In laughter and tears, we can our mountain climb.

When we are young and learn what is right
And feel the fear of life, when we set with blight
Then find the right from the wrong things done
But still in life, there can be lots of fun.

In our infant years we find no inhibitions,
Love is given freely to all, without condition.
So short this time in which we're giving trust
To every being - we feel that life is just.

We learn a little section of life each day
Sorting the good from the bad, and work from play.
The images we create in our small mind anew
Learning each day what's right for you.

In double figures we find a thing called youth,
Then all is revealed, and tell lies from the truth.
Then the transition from youth to full grown man
Going from school to find work, if we can.

The twenties take their toll on life it's true,
You think by now there is nothing to learn or do
In fact the opposite seems so true we see
Things are not the same as you thought they'd be

So life is an experience, that we all must learn.
And maybe to infancy, would we perhaps return
To be uninhibited, the way we were, before we grew,
To know yesterday's old, let tomorrows all renew.

Mike Lowe

THE PAST SPEAKS

The seconds of my life circle my head, while
The seconds of my future have become the wind,
Moving quickly and silently, unseen and fleeting.

I know that soon my time piece will slow and stop
Then die. And I will become just another memory,
A face on the wall, for a child to point and ask 'Who's that?'

Of my body, I have no children who use my name.
Yet I don't worry that I have no legacy to leave.
The fact that my name will die with me is of no bother,

Because people will remember me when they read my work.
My legacy you will find there. A legacy that will live
Longer than any child, found between the pages of a book.

My life will unfold to those people who care to look.
I am there, alive. My personality is tucked between chapters,
and the emotions I have felt through my life, are there to be experienced.

I die in peace.

Janet Lynn Craine

CHANGE

When we are children we don't worry at all
Our soul aim in life is to have a good time
The woes of the world, they pass us by
Our childhood, just one long nursery rhyme.

As we get older, so problems we find,
At home and at school then later at work
The stress and strain begin to tell,
And behind a facade of normality we lurk.

Frightened to change the life that we have.
The unknown more terrifying than the life we know.
To take those steps to change our ways,
A path down which we're frightened to go.

Decisions to make, choices to take,
Do we have the courage to make the change
Dare we settle for second best,
Or make a move to a life that's strange.

Denise Almond

HEADING FOR WHERE?

The wheels of time
on a rocky road
but where does it lead?
Where does it go?

Travelling and moving
from day to day
Maturing and growing
along the way.

Decisions and choices
at every turn
So much to look at
and so much to learn.

Where are we going,
the universe heart?
Or are we just circling
back to the start?

Searching for answers
is searching in vain
For these are the answers
you'll never obtain.

W V Ponting

BABY WANTS TO PLAY

Who cares about the ironing
What's a crease or two
I can see the sunshine smiling
When baby plays with you

The dust will always be there
The work will wait a day
But little baby's laughing
I know she wants to play

What will she remember
The beds so neatly made
Or the songs you sung together
The day that mummy played

Sally Frances Cazeaux

FREEZE FRAME

It's in the beginning, fresh and new,
A whole new life, a whole new view,
The world begins without a clue,
        The beginning of your life.

Then you grow, grow in an hour,
Life goes on so quickly not in power,
Life's blossoming grows every flower,
        The middle of your life.

Dying, an unlucky dying game,
The point of life? It's all the same,
The pleasures, the sadness, the christening name,
How can all the sadness equal fame,
        The dying, dying life.

K L Oldman

HIGH SCHOOL BLUES

Put clean undies on,
And brush your teeth,
Have you washed behind your ears?
Now comb your hair,
And clean your shoes,
You'll thank me in a few years.

Go to school,
Get good grades,
There's something nice for tea.
Don't spit at the teachers,
Or beat up your peers,
And don't you come crying to me!

Do this, do that,
Don't walk away,
I'm trying to talk to you.
You can't go out,
It's way too late,
You've homework left to do.

Don't pick your spots,
Or scratch your bum,
Ladies should always act nice.
Met your teachers again,
You've missed too may lessons,
And they're fed up of you picking fights.

Are you listening to me?
Are you alive today?
What time did you get home this morning?
You had better look lively,
Exam in ten minutes,
They disqualify students for snoring!

Daze Oakes

THE MIRROR

The mirror has reflected me
In oh so many ways
My childhood and my teenage years
On sad and happy days
The hairstyles and the fashions
The heartache and the pride
Until one day I looked in it
With my loved one by my side

And on my wedding day
In the mirror I could see
A happy smiling face
The mirror said was me
A year passed by
Our first born came
And soon came number two
And the reflection in the mirror said
Your daughter looks like you.

The years have gone by
For the mirror and me
I look in it now
And what do I see
A face that has cared through life's turbulent tide
And then once again my heart swelling with pride
I took my granddaughter on my knee
I looked in the mirror and what did I see
In the eyes of a child an image
And the image was of me.

Sheila Jessop

FORTY . . . SOMETHING

You wake up early and brush your hair,
Anti-cellulite your wrinkly face,
Although you've used almost one full gallon,
More wrinkles are appearing with great haste!

Next it's the bathroom to clean your teeth
While they're grinning at you through the glass,
You've flossed and waxed them but the plaque still attacked them,
And now they look at you and laugh!

Cos . . . When you turn forty things start falling apart,
    When you turn forty you still feel young at heart,
    When you turn forty your eyes and body sag,
      And some cheeky kid says 'You are a right 'Old Bag'.

Next it's Jane Fonda exercise
So bend and stretch and lean,
Just why is it that she does it easy?
While you roll around the floor and scream.
Now its aerobics, you ready for this?
Galop then Star jump in the air,
Now smile because it really hurts you
And I think you've torn your underwear!

When you've turned forty things are falling apart,
When you've turned forty you're still young at heart,
When you've turned forty your eyes and body sag,
But keep up the exercise
Cos . . . you'll drive your old man mad!

Heather Hasthorpe

FAMILY TREE

From the seeds of love it's grown.
With life and heartbeats of its own.
All sons and daughters mother earth embrace,
To grow in every country, with colour, type, and race.
God put it there for you and me.
It's the family tree.

Along its spreading branches,
The fruit of love are born to scatter on the field of life,
To grow like wheat and corn.
Some grow and thrive to splendour.
Some struggle in the mire.
But through it all the family tree,
With all its young inspire.

There is no limitation to its spreading fruiting style.
As long as love keeps feeding back to roots that are fertile.
Through trial and tribulations,
Or other forms of strife,
It can produce a harvest, for the process we call life,
And it's carried on through you and me,
With the family tree. . .

R Powell

FIRST LOVE

The little brook runs gently through
The fields where we once played
Its silver ripples echo out
The vows that we once made.

To come back when we'd grown up
When we knew what life's about
To laugh and sing along the banks
We couldn't be without.

It would be on a summer's eve
On that we did agree
But sadly you broke your promise
And it was left to only me.

The little brook still runs gently through
And I stand there on my own
Remembering the childhood love
Are you also quite alone?

Doris Moss

MIZPAH

Sorting possessions after death,
reveals the story of my incompleteness.
Slowly, silently, in a lonely house,
'She' emerges like petals from an unfurling bud.

Evidence of existence
revealed in parts:
a vanilla scented shawl,
a teddy bear in a drawer,
the tiny circlet of plastic,
laying bare her identity.

An image of a tiny form,
A date on the back of a sepia-coloured print,

      Stops my life force flowing.

      Now I know, I understand,

In finding you
I find myself,

The other part of me.

Geraldine Ann Howarth

THE GUESTS

The table's all set, best china laid out
Poor mam, she has slaved all day
Triangle sandwiches placed about in neat, precise array.

There's ham ones and egg ones
and some tomato and cheese,
And cake layers with cream and some jam,
'Bout' time I think for our guests to
arrive, then we can all eat ooh! Yes please
She wanders about, with 'that' look on
her face, there's something wring with our mam.

It can't be the food, and we've all been good,
So what could it possibly be?
She watches the clock, and hears it chime.
Which tells our mam it's now three.
But after a while she loses her smile.
The look on her face now says more.
She sits and she stares for what
seems to be a long while
That darned clock is now telling her four!

'They're not coming' I say,
'We've got the wrong day',
'Don't be silly,' Mam says
'I don't mix up my days!'
So into our note-pad I peek
'Mam the day is not wrong
'You were right, so you were'
'But now go and check on the week!'

Polly P

LIVING SHOCK

For a moment my heart jolted,
My lungs imploded.
And a single blip of silence
Moved across my head.

No air passed these lips,
My eyes rigid and transfixed,
And my stomach, gutted and empty
Fell at my feet.

Crumpled on the floor, occasionally
Capable of sighing.
A day passed, or was it a year?
It's warm outside and I'm still here.

Clover Peake

CIRCLES OF FREEDOM

Often I think where does the circle begin and end
Then what does it matter if we do not comprehend.
As the Olympic flag with its interlocking rings
Flies overhead, spirits are raised every heart sings.

A sudden tumultuous cheer echoes all around
Contestants line up, although no feet will touch the ground.
The wheelchair race, with a few obstacles thrown in too
Is about to start, everyone waiting for the cue.

I realise now as I concentrate on the course
Long gone are the black days when I felt utter remorse.
My two sturdy circles have opened up a new world
Like the Olympic flag overhead I feel unfurled.

Mary E Beale

APPLE BLOSSOMS

There was an apple tree in the garden
In the place we used to pay,
Blossom petals like avalanches
In the early days of May,
Like fairy wings, rose tipped and scented
In the garden we frequented,
Long ago.

The swing was high
And we could try
To make our toes reach the sky
And who would know?

Autumn came and a wishing well
Near where the rosy apples fell
An old old water pump
And a sun flower standing high!
How has heaven escaped us now
When it was there in days gone by?

Joan Bayley

POMP AND CIRCUMSTANCE

Strutting like a prize peacock
He makes his presence felt
His entourage assume it's dead-lock
In whose mouth butter wouldn't melt.

The hingers on wait on his every word
As if it had been sculptured by hand
He is as far as they are concerned a lord
When he oversees his land.

Honesty and integrity are his bread and butter
Although some around are heard to mutter
Subversives are not playing cricket
More than likely they'll be pickets

Reality dramatically appears
And with it all those unfounded fears
Sober as a judge
Left with no issues to fudge
Homeward safely they all trudge.

Alastair Buchanan

NANA DIED ON THURSDAY

Nana died on Thursday, Michael phoned me up at school,
He'd had an urgent message, he ignored them as a rule,
She'd called us out so often with pains that were not there.
The Doctor said she'd feigned them, though they were the worst she'd swear
Her stomach gave her problems, her headaches were severe,
But her heart it was the strongest so we were not to fear.
And yet they found her sitting, the radio blasting forth,
Her teacup on the carpet, while she sat on the hearth.
They said that she felt nothing, her heart had simply failed,
Yet we both felt guilty, as we stood there shocked and paled.
We'd given her such a talking to about how she should try
To make an effort, join a club, we never thought she'd die!
She was here for lunch on Sunday, on Monday she was pale,
Tuesday we walked her round the green, Wednesday, though feeling frail
Our advice she meekly took and to the Warden's party went,
So our evening visit we forsook and now we sit here grieving
As we never saw her more, her little home we're emptying,
Treasured scatters near and far
Her funeral is on Monday, grandsons bear her to the grave,
Family friends will mourn with us for a generation passed away.

Avrille Oxley McCann

THE CIRCLE OF LIFE

Congratulations! You're a new mother
And very soon you will discover
Nappies, bottles and safety pins
And a hundred other strange new things.

A few faltering steps, your toddler takes.
And mother's there to see he's safe
To pick him up when he's fallen down
Bathe his knee and soothe his frown.

The telephone rings or a neighbour calls
Mother looks round, and they've crayoned the walls
A smack bottom follows, and she puts them to bed
And they end up crayoning the bedroom instead.

He's started school so tall and smart
And another string pulls on a mother's heart
At the school gates mother waves goodbye
She says 'Be Brave' but it's her to cry

The years speed on and they're in their teens
It's all pop records and tight blue jeans
A mother's old fashioned when she worries and waits
She said ten thirty and they're half an hour late.

When romance is over and advice goes unheeded
It's a mother's love that's sorely needed
A shoulder to cry on, a cuddle, a friend
Someone to tell her it's not quite the end.

It's wedding bells ringing, and choir boys singing
A mother's heart breaking, a new start awakening
It's time to let go - it's their life together
But the ties of a mother no one can sever.

A new baby's crying and grandmother's sighing.
And nothing's quite lost in a mother's pure love
The circle's unending like God's love in sending
A new generation, for us to love.

Carol Burton

THE CIRCLE OF LIFE

Fashioned from clay
Out of Round planet earth
The sweet breath of life -
Miraculous birth.
Here starts the circle -
But who knows the end?
Who are we mortals,
To comprehend?

The life-giving rays
Of the circular sun,
Nurturing, nourishing everyone.
But not so, it seems
In the countries where they
Feel the sun's rays - day after day.
A terrible drought overtakes the land,
Sorrowful eyes, and outstretched hands.

We all have our circles
Of various size.
There's no way of knowing,
And there's no prize
For the one who lives the longest -
Or the one who's here least,
The circle keeps turning -
For man and for beast.

Iona James

TIME FOR ALL

Grandfather clock stands in the hall
It's been there two hundred years, it has seen all
The changes that have come along
As it tells every hour with a chime
But nothing has changed for this old clock
Still playing the game of time
Time to get up, time to go to bed
Time to be born, time to be dead
Time for everything for us to choose it
But it doesn't tell us how to use it
It doesn't make night, it doesn't make day
But puts down a marker in case we delay
Time doesn't have a fast or a slow
Its up to ourselves which way we go
If we can't go slow, or can't go fast
Don't worry, time has passed
Passed us all and always will
It's us that are moving and time's standing still
If this grandfather clock has told me a tale
I'm as wise at first as at last
If time standing still, it gives me a chill
To think it's me and the clock that have passed.

P W W

CIRCLE OF LIFE

Birth, fills a man, and woman with great joy,
Then childhood, has its fair share of strife.
Trials, and heartache for both girl and boy,
When embarking on his eternal circle of life.

First it is school then the starting of toil.
Next comes true love, for a man and his wife.
Working in factory, office, tilling the soil,
Striving hard to maintain his circle of life.

Age catches up so fast, he is forced to retire,
Death comes sudden, like the thrust of a knife.
He maybe buried in earth, consumed by the fire,
But he has simply fulfilled his circle of life.

A C Spindler

THREE SCORE YEARS AND THIRTY

I had to let her go, I couldn't carry on.
Sleepless nights and day jobs, finally took their toll.
She fell, she lost her way, she left the water on,
She couldn't even dress herself, her mind had completely gone.

Seventeen years she'd lived with us but I don't regret a one.
She was trying, she was tying, especially as the years rolled on.
I miss her more than words can say
And wish she hadn't gone.

At eighty-eight she had to go, we couldn't carry on.
It was a time of turmoil - how could we let her go
To live with strangers she didn't know, who didn't know her ways,
Who couldn't love her as we did and care about her woes.

She has no teeth, she has no specs and only knows the time
To eat when she is hungry and sleep when she is tired.
She broke her hip, she cut her eye and falls from out her cot.
She doesn't know me half the time but I love her an awful lot.

And now she's nearly ninety!
Why do I have to grieve - so much for someone not yet gone?
Because she is my Mother and the memories linger on -
Of what she was and what she is and what will be the end.
God only knows when that will be, perhaps when I am gone.

E P Leek

MY FATHER

He started to go grey on the day I was born
He told me that one day in our garden on the lawn
'When you were just a little child
You often made me really wild.'

Well I remember being put across his knee.
The neighbours must have thought he was killing me!
He even had a cane on a shelf above the door.
He told me once that it was there
And what he'd used it for . . .
The one fine day I broke the cane for ever,
And never did he mention it again - no never . . .

Dad had a dreadful temper, but could also be so kind.
Eventually I decided that I really didn't mind
His anger which on me was so very often vent.
My life was really quite secure
And I was well content.

At night I was so nervous of the dark and had a light,
Until my parents went to bed, and then it was all right.
In my bedroom when I heard dad's most resounding snore,
I had the reassurance that he was just next door.

Unfortunately my father's greatest love was food.
He ignored the doctors' warnings and got in a bad mood,
When at fifteen stone my mother tried
to make him lose some weight,
He really got quite angry and soon it was too late.

He was struck down by thrombosis and we lost him in his prime.
But he lived on in our memories
And we talked of happy times
When father's sense of humour made each day a happy day.
These are the kind of memories that will never pass away

Barbara R Thompson

THE ROAD TO RETIREMENT

At twenty, I taught in a suburban school, seven year old boys full of fun,
Two years later, teaching English and RE, to a Girls' School I went.
Nine years pass and in a Comprehensive School teaching boys and girls
                                                                    I'd begun.
Year Co-ordinator in a City School, three very full years there I spent.
Next to Somerset as Deputy Head in a town unlike Liverpool!
Then off to the Midlands I went to teach English in a Girls' Public School.

Four more years in a Midland Primary School, two followed as Deputy Head,
Next, I was appointed a Middle School Head, in Staffordshire's fair
                                                                    County town.
A Headship soon in another Middle School was where my career had led.
The it finally came, the glorious day, the reins of control I laid down!
My retirement came and I whooped with joy at the thought of the
                                                                    time I knew
That I'd have to spend any way I chose on the things I wanted to do.

But retirement days are as full as ever; it's beyond me to tell you how
To prepare and teach I could ever find time, and it's not many years ago.
Church meetings to go to and also to Chair, and Minutes I have
                                                                    to write - now!
Lessons in swimming for my husband and I, with grandchildren also we go
And three days a week, the house is alive with grandchildren's'
                                                                    cheerful voices.
There are letters to read, poems to write, so many exciting choices.

This list isn't finished as I also go to my well-loved women's meeting,
On the central committee I said I'd serve, so I go around the county.
I know the joy of a glorious garden, which needs much hoeing and weeding!
But then there's the garden swing to relax in, from where I survey my bounty!
A hectic life of retirement I lead, thought one of pleasure and splendour,
So I count my blessings and shout for joy as my daily thanks I render.

Sheila E Harvey

147

THE TEENAGER

They go to bed at twelve years old,
All smiles and hugs and curls.
Overnight the child mutates,
And a teenager unfurls.
They're sullen and they're grumpy,
They pay their music loud.
Do just what their pals do,
To be in with the crowd.
Untidy and uncivil,
The world is on their case.
Their temper is as volatile
As the spots upon their face.
You're! Treated like an alien,
They're! Always highly strung.
You wouldn't understand them,
As if you were never young.
Now as a teenager's parent,
I have to say in truth.
If I'd known how hard the job was,
I'd have been a better youth . . .

John A Young

CIRCLES

What a simply charming sight,
When shopping, in noon of day.
See aged pair, with bits and bobs,
Still much in love, with hand in hand.

Of course my dear, you are so right.
Indeed, they need somewhere to play.
Concern for people, for little jobs,
To care, to help, to understand.

Is youth wasted on the young?
In truth, it's theirs by right.
Flaming passion, aroused and gone,
Caressed by noise and flashing light.

The *wash of time*, refreshes as we wilt,
The *mule* and the *donkey*, finally learn.
The good we do, resolves the guilt,
This way out, is just, return.

Peter Barton

THE LIVING DEPTHS OF MAN ...

Within the living depths of man,
There is a time for all -
The gentleness of springtime,
The sorrow of the fall,
The heat and light of summer,
The harsh and stark of frost,
The mellow fires of winter,
Showing all is never lost,
The crash and fire of mighty storms -
With tears that lie withal,
The glowing tones of summer,
A lovers beckoning call,
The breeze across the ocean,
An ever sweet caress,
The lightening of the heavens,
Making human sorrows less . . .
Within the living depths of man,
There is a time for all,
The lives and loves and melodies
From time beyond recall . . .

Anna Hooton

ELEGY

'Tis true, he waits for no man,
his hands must touch us all,
awake, asleep, come hither reap,
and listen to his call.

They set aside a plot of land,
within the cemetery,
a shallow berth of common earth,
in which they buried me.

They made a handsome coffin,
oh hapless wooden cell!
Along with me, 'twill buried be,
condemned to die as well.

A marble slab upon my head,
a touching floral wreath,
this sign of life bodes man and wife
to death that lies beneath.

Their duties now completed,
the mourners leave my side,
their love may earn a brief return,
still sad that I have died.

A vigil, too, perhaps they'll tend,
a Sabbath of their own,
a heart's decree to honour me,
who sleepeth here alone.

They may bring fresher flowers,
and put them on my grave,
a tear to cry, beloved I,
the one they could not save.

Yet these unleashed emotions,
be they false or be sincere,
no good to me, for can't you see,
I am dead, and cannot hear.

Lawrence Mentesh

THE LIFE CYCLE
(Dedicated to a devoted mother, Patricia Bell)

The frightened screams echo round the nursery
the relieved sighs echo round the ward
tears of love and joy leave mum's eyes
A new father expresses his pride

The laughs of celebration echo round the hall
Worried words echo round the house
Streamers and music clash in excitement
the child becomes an adult

The wedding bells echo round the church
Cries of happiness echo round the ceremony
Vows of honesty are sealed not to be broken
two hearts are joined as one

Sobs of unhappiness echo round the cemetery
Deathly uneasiness fills the air
A loved one has reached the end
A tired soul is put to rest

The frightened screams echo round the nursery
the relieved sighs echo round the ward
tears of love and joy leave mum's eyes
A new father expresses his pride

Dawn Louise Bell

MY TEENAGE YEARS

My teenage years, were the best years for me.
They were filled with laughter, merriment, and glee
I remember at sixteen, being given the chance
To visit the church hall, to attend the weekly dance.

'Jiving' 'Jitterbugging', enjoying myself, the whole night long,
When it was over, I wondered, where the time had gone.
Of course in those days, I could stay to the end.
Because the dance hall opened seven until ten.

I had shoes, with high heels, for the very first time.
Those black patent ones, was a great favourite of mine.
'Make up' too, I was allowed to use, but just a little touch.
Powder, lipstick, mascara and rouge, to give my cheeks a rosy blush.

Even now, at this present time.
I remember that little black dress of mine
With a string of pearls, earrings that matched as well
I used to wonder, who'll ask me to dance, but only time would tell.

Those Friday night dances, in the years that have passed.
Brought me many memories, that will always last.
How I wish I could still be one of the first, through those big doors,
To try out, and practice new steps, on that beautiful polished floor.

I find it funny now, talking with friends of my own age,
They didn't think that Ballroom Dancing was worth learning at that stage.
So my advice to anyone who has yet, to learn how to dance,
Dancing is enjoyment, good exercise, great fun, so please take a chance.

G Chamberlain

SONNET TO SENILITY

Valentine's Day has come and gone
But I'm still waiting here alone.
No one has called me on the phone.
The total of my cards is none.
What a change from days gone by!
I was used to making hay
With lovers who would sob and sigh
If I refused to make their day.
Anyone who is past his prime,
Frail and slow, and somewhat lame,
Can only dream, and pass his time
Remembering his fleeting fame.
Carefree youth is quickly past.
Oblivion beckons at the last.

Frank Henry

REALITY

Where is my love
    That I no longer see
Her gentle touch and fond embrace
    Is but a memory.
Times we discussed a life
    In higher sphere,
Of death we talked
    But in agreement - Not to fear.
We pictured 'After Life'
    As what we thought and read,
The question asked -
    And in reply I said.
'Where on Earth can Heaven be?
    - For sure it's where
    You are with me!'

T G Bloodworth

OLD AGE

What's to become of me?
Old age won't let me wander free.
Couped up in this old armchair,
Can't even open a window for a breath of air!

Having to ask for everything,
Even the toilet nurse has to bring.
How I long to get up and go.
To see the friend I used to know.

Now long since dead, and without care.
Waiting for me over there.
Why I'm left here I do not know.
What did I do wrong? to suffer so.

I ask this question many times.
And now I can't think of a word that rhymes!

George William Bailey

ANOTHER WORLD

There's another world comes after this
One free of misery and pain
You will cast off your tired body
And you'll be young again

There are summer skies of limpid blue
Fields of the softest green
Light filled flowers of every hue
Such as you have never seen

When you walk through that door of purest gold
Say goodbye to all sin and care
It's true my friend, believe me it's true
I know because I've been there.

Margaret Eva Colley

ANGER AT LIFE

Who said life was so meaningful?
It just strained my body,
And drained my mind,
All the thoughts I have lived,
Will be lost in this land of time.

Why, is your mind not twisted?
You have not been affected by time,
Effortlessly living, but without any body.
My body and mind are still here,
But not sweet in living,
Creating unbeknown silence,
But I am still here.

I will take light from others,
And hold it within my grasp,
Tightening a vengeful fist,
For I'll spread none like this.
My greed was wanting to be loved,
A pitiful thoughtfulness,
That my mind could not erase.

Let the depths confront us,
There's no excusing,
Let our limits be broken,
With no understanding,
Let our presence elude us,
Without confrontation.
But should we need correctiveness,
Let it come in colours.

Richard Bright

SCHOOL - LEAVER'S ACRONYM
(To everyone at the Denes High School, 1992 - 1996)

T oday I am leaving, and I'm
H appy to say, I've enjoyed my time here in
E very way.
D espite all those subjects I'd rather not
E ver learn, my hard work paid off and I went on to learn a
N ice string of grades, mostly As, B, and Cs,
E ven if there's more to life than GCSEs. The
S ixth form for instance is worth living through - it's not all
H ard work, there's pool and parties too.
I n conclusion I'd say that I'm
G lad to
H ave been one of those who've grown up through the
S chool they
C all Denes. The best days of my life? Well, it's hard to see
H ow they could be bettered, I have to agree. And
O n leaving the Denes let me say
O nce again that I'd give my years here at
L east ten out of ten.

Claire Handscombe

GOODBYE

Don't weep for me when I am dead,
Some words are better left unsaid,
I'll live on in your heart and mind,
And in memories of the nicer kind.

Don't pity me when I am gone,
For when I bid this world 'So long,'
Away so far will fly my soul,
In the search to find another role.

Don't cry, or say that life's unfair,
For it won't be me who's lying there,
My spirit will be upwards bound,
Before my bones are underground.

So on the evening of my death,
When I submit my final breath,
Look up into the twinkling light,
For there'll be an extra star that night.

Rachael Doherty

MOTHER'S LOVE

Sitting beside the open fire
Waiting for my bath.
Gazing at our kid getting scrubbed.
Hearing my mother laugh.

Drying him off, then on her knee,
Scurf comb through his hair.
No nits tonight, a gentle kiss.
A smack on his bottom bare.

We empty the bath, me and mam,
Out the back, down the sink.
Mamma gives a nod and a smile,
It's my turn now, I think.

Into the bath I jump with glee,
A quick scrub down, then on her knee,
A million pound, I would not miss,
For her gentle touch, and tender kiss.

Up the dancers now to sleep
Then mam pops up, to have a peep
Quietly off to bed she will go,
God Bless You Mum. I love you so.

Harlequin

YOUTH

'Youth' that's the golden glow
Looking back we ought to know
Thrill that you are just sixteen
Attractive centre of the scene

The world your oyster, take the pearl
Grasp it tight, give life a whirl
Nothing barred all to gain
Live and love, go for fame

This slice of life, these years so few
Make them count, it's up to you
If you stall at youth's door
Sad regrets forever more.

C Cox

THIRD SPRING FOR HEIDRUN

The throbbing grass
The cold oily sweat
Under melting glaciers
Under avalanches of lust
I sharpen my fingernails
After spring's coarse laughter
To wind over mountain lakes
And see
Two bodies defying the elements
Beside the choking sea
The diamond sand
Two pairs of eyes descending
Clashing like waves over seaweed
Against all odds
Merging
Into a symphony of birth

Robert Hrdina

ADOLESCENCE

Spotty face,
Spiked red hair,
Flared blue faded jeans
Worse for wear,
Irritable, stubborn and stroppy
Life's not what it seems,
Adolescents have a head
Full of wonderful dreams

C Baldam

LIFE AND DEATH

The old man told me
'Living is more punishment than death'
I did not understand
How could this be?
With each day
Was an adventure
A struggle for survival
Each day, every day
Survival was purely a chance
Death on the other hand
Was an ultimate chance of peace
The final peace
Peace one rarely finds
Until the final goodbye, the final farewell
Peace when living, one rarely, one never finds.

Kauser Parveen

MUM AND DAD

You have always been there,
When I have needed you most.
And so from me to you,
I shall make a little toast.

Thank you both for everything,
Especially your endless love.
And teaching me what's right from wrong,
Which must have proved quite tough.

Your smiles make me happy,
When I was feeling sad.
And punishments made me realise,
It isn't good to be bad.

You fed me well and cared for me,
And put a roof over my head.
And I will always remember how,
You'd tuck me into bed.

I love you mum and dad,
More than words can ever say.
This will never change because,
My love is here to stay.

Leah Taylor

THE PATCHWORK QUILT

Look back sometimes,
and you will find
a unique patchwork quilt

The brightest square
is waiting there,
for you to see and hold

Some patches fray,
parts wear away,
but threads bind them together

Reach out and touch,
they mean so much,
you *are* the living fabric

Sheila M Churchill

OLD

When youth is gone and we grow old,
Lots of tales we do unfold.
Of days gone by of prices not so high,
Of longer Summers and blue skies.

Some people tell of the War so long,
Of closer people and singalongs,
How they help each other when times were bad,
A smile at a neighbour made a sad heart glad.

Days when doodlebug bombs did fall from the sky,
Sadness when a friend did die.
To find your house blown apart a must to make you cry.
Then a neighbour would take you in,
And wipe the tear from your eye.

A pint of beer was only a shilling you'd hear them say
in them good old days,
When friendly coppers roamed the streets,
and the sun had warmer rays.

Yes age some of us it makes us wise,
Though some old ones are quick to criticise,
So enjoy the days as they unfold,
and you might be wise as you grow old.

D Rowlinson

THE BEGINNING
(Dedicated To Daniel)

I have to admit it's been cosy in here,
Warm and secure with nothing to fear,
She's nice - that lady that's carrying me,
But I'm ready now - I want to be free.

Just to let her know I give a little kick,
Yet all it seems to do is make the nice lady sick,
Oh! There's a nice man too (he puts his head on her tummy)
And keeps saying things like 'Nearly time Mummy!'

Who are these people? - I really don't know,
But they keep feeding me up and helping me grow,
I'm getting too large now to live in this space,
Time to prepare for showing my face.

Oh no! The nice lady's screaming in pain,
I didn't realise this would cause such a strain,
So I hold back a little (she's been good after all)
But she pushes even harder and I start to fall.

Then with one final incredible push,
I leave my world behind in quite a rush,
I'm not sure if I like it out here,
It's all very big and unclear.

They shout 'It's a boy!'
And give me a slap,
Then as I start to cry,
They start to clap!

They place me gently in that 'Mummy person's' arms
I was right about her - she has certain charms,
As she smiles at me it all becomes clear,
As I snuggle in I know I'm going to like it out here.

A M Carr

MUGGED

Here I am alone and scared,
Waiting to hear that someone cares,
I have lots of friends or so I thought,
But no one has bothered to see if I am alright,
After I had a terrible fright,
When someone mugged me the other night,
He said he had a knife,
I thought he was going to take away my life,
I keep thinking he still might,
Now I'm jumping at every sound,
Just in case he has come round.
I wish he could feel this way,
Feeling scared every minute of the day.

Amanda Jervis

FACE TO FACE

I look in the mirror, what do I see?
A wrinkled old lady. Can it be me?
I don't feel old, I'm young at heart
It's how others see me that tears me apart
So I'll turn the mirror to the wall
Although it's only me that I can fool
Now I can skip and dance, play in the fields
Climb the trees, go head over heels
I was once young, pretty and free
I like to think that is still me
The knowledge and know-how is stored in my mind
By and large nature has been kind
I turn the mirror round, have another look
What do I see - a well read book

Gladys C'Ailceta

BRETON MAGIC

Through Fouesnant forest we slid down
Empty ribbons by dark trees.
I followed him across a bridge
At Josselin where women crouched at midday
Washing linen at the water's edge.
Lace caps and lizards, bagpipes and the bay
Black with seaweed and at night
We trailed through orchards crowned
With mistletoe, down to the beach and heard
A friend singing a Russian lullaby,
Parting the air; a magic time.
Under hot canvas in a tent of gold
As July ends beneath old apple trees
We lay in morning love and our child began.

Mary Barry

STANDSTILL

I have too much going on in my head
That needs to be resolved
Too much excess baggage
That suddenly built up
Perhaps unintentionally over time
That have remained unresolved
That have remained untouched
But I wasn't ready
But I wasn't equipped
With skills, with knowledge, with experience
Now I stand prepared
To shrug some of it off
So I can start to grow
Again.

Naeem Mirza

MONUMENT II

Massive against the skyline's glare,
a legend cast in stone,
a presence of a presence,
atop my skin and bone.
When first they laid me down to rest
you were shiny, black and new,
soon I began to change a little
and so in time, did you.
A little moss, a little weed,
the grass a little overgrown,
and me a little different,
from solid flesh to hollow bone.
Another year or thereabouts,
it's pretty hard to tell,
most of me is hard to find
but you're still looking well.
No-one to visit, no-one to see
all things I guess must pass,
but the words are there for all to read
and at least they cut the grass.
More time flies by and back you lean,
the earth is moving on,
and now when people pass me by
you're here whilst I am gone.
And now the end but not for you,
your stone heart beats out the age,
you were the book and library
whilst alas I only a page.

Mark Julian Morris

THE FANTASY OF DREAMS

Under the nameless conductor
the galactic orchestra performs
the music of the spheres,
as the dominating rhythms
penetrate the essence of mankind
pulsating deep into our brains,
our minds, our spirits and our souls.

And now the dreamfire
of the burning bush
is blazing to illuminate
the long dark night of man
with dreams of life, love,
care, hope, fellowship and pity
and true compassion for all life.

With the intruding light of dawn
he opens his reluctant eyes
and resentfully awakes
into his sleeping dozing life
as the chill bleak wind of day
invades and all his holy dreams sink
into the vortex of the lifeless world.

Stephen Gyles

EVERLASTING LIFE

To never see again your face,
Long disappeared without a trace,
Has left in me, an empty space,
      Finality.

Yet in the mirror I can see
Your features looking back at me,
A cutting from the family tree,
      Heredity.

And in my children's traits do I
Your looks and character espy,
For legacies within us lie,
    Immortality.

D T Morgan

NEVER-ENDING CHAIN

Born - a new baby for our mum
A gooy goo and some and some
Christopher spent hours in his cot
Wearing dirty nappies before he learnt to use the pot
Then with my help he began to crawl then walk
And one day to my surprise he began to talk
He used to follow me everywhere
Whenever I turned around he was sure to be there
School seemed to catch him up quite soon
And then he was singing a different tune
He was clever like me and passed his eleven plus
And every day we caught the same bus
He even ended up at my old college to learn how to cook
And I smiled and giggled and stuck my head in a book
When he left, with honours, I got him into my hotel
And for a long long time we both worked at the Bell
He even decided to get married on the same day as me
And we both have boys who are now in 2B
But when Mum and Dad died we were both very sad
For they were the very best friends Christopher and I had
    ever had
But such I guess is the circle of life
And we must both be grateful for our family and wife.

Cherry Somers-Dowell

HELTER SKELTER

Mummy took me to the fair
all the children smiled,
She took me to the helter skelter
where all the children gathered.
I, like the others started a slow ascent.
When I reached the fourth step,
I had finished lower school,
by the time I reached the eighth,
I was looking for employment,
my wife and children joined me
as I climbed onto the twelfth.
On the sixteenth step my children left,
on the twentieth my wife died.
I reached the top, tired and lonely,
laid down and rested my eyes.
The descent was fast and I
felt so refreshed, so I started
to climb again.

Wayne Ford

STAGES OF LIFE

As a baby into the world you came,
You grew and as a child you played the game.
As years go by teenage years come and go.
You meet someone special and love just grows.

You become an adult and marry one another
A home maker you became, and also a mother
You bring up a family and one day they have flown
You and your husband are left on your own.

As years fly by and age creeps on
You make another life for yourselves, youth gone
Then one day you're left all on your own
No-one to talk to, only the use of the phone.

Mavis P Morrey

A FOOL IN HIS TIME

Where's all the time gone that I once had,
It was only yesterday when I was a lad,
What's happened to dreams of life after school,
To all of those schemes, was I just a fool?

Earning my living to reap what I've sown,
But what were they giving, no more than was owed.
For a pittance of pay I worked like a mule,
'Til retirement day, just like a fool.

I married my lady who gave me much joy,
She bore me a baby, a beautiful boy,
But he died, still a baby, life is so cruel,
It drove me half crazy, this tormented fool.

My lady turned away and left me all alone,
I pleaded with her to stay but she turned to stone.
She passed away without a word, gone my precious jewel,
Wanting her back is absurd, I am the lonely fool.

My mind is still eager but my body is unable,
My movements a meagre shuffle across to the table.
Life is nearing its end so existing is the only rule,
My ailments won't mend so good-bye from the fool.

Philip Quinton Mills

THE CIRCLE OF LIFE

Travelling round at constant speed,
the circle of life has no ending.
People get on and others get off.
Time is inflexible, never bending.

We say how quickly the day has gone,
depends what we have in mind,
working 'gainst time to finish a job
there's no extra minutes to find.

Do we travel round the circle?
Or does it spin and take us round?
In good times do we go round faster?
Spinning on with scarce a sound.

Is the circle here forever?
From man's dawning to his end.
You can't get off to take a breather
or slow down for there is no bend.

We join the circle when we're born
and travel round for life.
School, work and growing older
in a world so full of strife.

If fortunate we find good friends
to join us through the years
and travel with them by our side
to share our hopes and fears.

Now we are reduced to two,
our family scattered wide.
We still cling to the wheel of life
just we two side by side.

D Jennings

LIFE ANALYSED

Basically it is a set routine
And well yes always has it been
Night follows day and day does night
The spinning earth's the reason right

Morning time you get out of bed
Night time it's rest your weary head
Each day you tend to do the same
Like that, seems tame this living game

Well not at all how soon we find
And all because we've got a mind
Inside the head so we can't doff
And never ever is switched off

Of course it's a workaholic
Like the heart but more sophistic
Never do we feel it working
Though our life it is enriching

Perception of each worldly thing
Also fine dreams emanating
Are tempered to our moods and selves
Perhaps no further should we delve

It's from here your ways are programmed
Outside forces should not be slammed
Really you do have some control
It's from the depths you call the soul.

H C Derx

AUTUMN'S CURTAIN

The autumn leaves come tumbling down,
Lovely shades, red, green and brown,
This will happen to you and me,
As God intended it to be,

We start so small, like little roots,
Then we grow strong and sturdy shoots,
Mother nature will have her way,
Little by little, day by day.

Not everyone beautiful or perfectly shaped,
But a charming character in sincerity draped,
Is sought after as much, if not more,
We've all something to offer, that's for sure.

When we are young, eager and free,
We bend with the wind, like a slender young tree,
With time roots grow deeper, we're harder to budge,
So set in our ways, until the occasional nudge.

Then suddenly we find, it's the autumn of life,
We look back on our happy days, struggle and strife,
It's time to let go, not afraid to be old,
Autumn leads to heaven, of beauty untold.

Eileen Handley

THE CIRCLE OF LIFE

Life begins at forty so many people say
getting more tired by the end of the day.
Time to spend on your own at last,
middle age is catching up fast.
The family being more independent,
makes you feel that you're redundant.
Perhaps at work you're more relaxed,
coming home to make the snacks.

Maybe gardening is your pleasure
taking time and make it leisure,
Having your hair in a new style maybe,
a facial is a treat you'll see.
Bracing walks can bring results.
Aerobics, yoga or keep-fit vaults.
There may be grandchildren to keep
                              you on your toes,
So live it up and forget your woes.

Mary Harris

CIRCLE OF LIFE

The spring bears newness and hope
As the innocent are born.
Like the spring you give joy and pride
Now you are given the gift of life.
You grow, mature and learn
As the summer sun begins,
You bloom like a rose in full dress
For all, like you, learn to love and respect.
As autumn approaches and the sun fades
The childhood and youth
Are all a memory to your age.
For now the darkness falls
So sudden on all of us, for life
It is the circle, we are to draw.
Slowly, like the flower
The life begins to fade,
That once was a bud, to
The beauty that summer had made.
The sun has faded
The nights begin to creep in,
From the day life was born
We now close the chapter of life
As the circle is fully drawn.

Anita Hanson

ELISA MAY NEAME

Congratulations Nessa!
Congratulations John!
I'd only been in bed an hour
When we were called upon,

To send a baby-sitter
O'er to Stone Street Farm
To make sure grandson Oliver
Did not come to harm.

The service will of course cost more
Because we had no warning
'Specially as the phone bell rang
At three o'clock this morning!

I'm glad this last month's over
The phone just drove me batty!
Each time it rang I said, 'That's Ness!'
And Carole got quite ratty.

'I just wish you'd stop saying that,
You really are a pain!'
'So Ness, I hope we can relax
'Til you produce again!

Our first grand-daughter's pretty cute
With the Cole's neat nose
It's frightening to think she may
Grow up with Neame big toes!

We're really happy for you three
Now you've got Elisa
So it's love from Carole and
The poem making geezer!

The Stowting Poet

174

EARLY RETIREMENT

I said farewell to the daily round,
the morning travel into town,
folks cautioned me, 'Its quiet at home,
you could be lost and all alone.'
I've missed my work pals it is true,
but my, the things I've found to do.

A tricky task is to unwind,
after years of slog and grind,
it's second nature, bustle, flurry,
a built in habit, always hurry.
I try to saunter round the shops,
no need to pull out all the stops.

Now I've found it such a treat,
to chat with people in the street,
not simply pass the time of day,
then have to rudely dash away.
It still seems strange and new to me,
to have or visit friends for tea,
a weekend date I'd always seek,
but never any in the week.

A working life has little time,
to have one's fill of summer's clime.
Contentedly I took full stock,
without that paymaster, the clock.
Although it's still a novelty,
forward looking I can see,
no matter if you're green or wise,
life will always bring surprise.

Ivy Wood

DEDICATED TO ALL IN DUNBLANE

That terrible day
In the town of Dunblane,
People hurt with desperation,
Lives will never be the same.

It was a normal day,
When you all went into class,
But you all didn't realise
How long it would last.

A strange man came in
With hate in his eyes.
Three minutes later
Most of you died.

The shots that were fired,
Who knows what you thought,
Fear and destruction
This man had brought.

We pray for your families,
To help their pain cease
And all your little children
Now rest in peace.

Kelly Morris (15)

ROLL-UP! ROLL-UP!

Yellow stains upon my hands,
Brown dots adorn my smile.
Eyes bloodshot from smoky clouds,
My breath is none but vile.

'It's my only vice,' is often said,
By smoke signals from afar.
Leave me alone, to slowly fill,
My lungs with sticky tar.

Take my legs, replace my parts,
My arteries have died.
Don't you fret, 'cause I am happy,
With my nicotine inside.

Then it comes, the final day,
And through your tears you spoke.
'It's goodbye from the crematorium,'
As I go up in smoke.

John Kelly

TEARS OF HOPE

When the sun slowly slides down the fading life screen,
old and bad times are nothing new, to this ancient world,
dark clouds disappear into the celestial void, unseen,
remembering all our youth, innocent days of boy and girl,
from womb to tomb, is the endless cycle of all our lives,
live and die, we know not why, these answers, we'll never know,
pleasure and pain, is always our gain, throughout we strive,
win or lose, what we learn about ourselves, is what we show,
violence and intolerance is always to be expected today,
invasion of property and of your person, peace deprived,
fear for yourself and the unknown, is the norm, try to allay,
it is always worth the lifetime struggle, fight to survive,
the dread of death is the only true fear, live with it to live,
be what you are, and be proud of yourself, whoever you may be,
a soul without terror is a heart without feeling or drive,
live life for you, in the circle of life, see what you can see,
never encroach into the well being of others, sowing evil seeds,
bad is bad, and not black or white, good is good, right is right,
all of us are equal to others, show this with rightful deeds,
life cycles began at the dawn of time, that is our worldly plight.

Josephine Elliott

DAD'S OLD CARDIGAN

I see you have still left it there Mum
Dad's old cardigan, hanging on the wall
Why do you keep that old worn out thing
It is not of much use, to anyone at all

You have given away all his shirts and ties
His suits his coats and trilby hat
You gave all his clothes away Mum
Why ever, do you keep that

Mum looked at me with saddened eyes
And in them welled the tears
It was always Dad's favourite
I won't throw it out, after all these years

The times I asked Dad to discard it
It's as good as new he always said
When it's washed, a couple of buttons
And seam stitched with matching thread

But all down the front is full of holes
Burnt by that awful pipe you smoke
It makes you look just like a tramp
And that is not a joke

He would wink and smile at me
His smile I loved so true
His wink and smile would melt my heart
Go on you wear it then, what else could I do

That's why it hangs in the hallway
Bringing memories of how happy we used to be
And when it comes my time to go
Bring it from the hallway, and place it next to me

Frederick Sowden

TADPOLES

They struggle for life these little things

They are jelly at first
Scooped from one place to another

So few survive
But when they do they are little black dots
With tiny tails
They live in a kingdom all of their own

The strong survive
The weak are eaten alive

As the weeks turn to months
They swim about their kingdom
Slowly turning into tiny frogs no bigger than a finger nail

Soon, though so small they can jump out of their kingdom
and explore
They sit out on the stones anxiously watched by the gardener
Who loves them like his own
So many are dried up in the sun, stuck to the stones

The garden despairs of any surviving
But somehow they do

They hibernate during the winter
And the circle of life starts again and again and again . . .

Rosalind Gearon

HAS THERE EVEN BEEN A SPARK?

Some days I find that life's not good
And I would end it if I could
The things I try will not work out
So I wonder what it's all about.

Would it change things overall
Had I not been born at all
Or should I die by some mishap
Would my going leave a gap.

Am I part of some great scheme
(That might help my self esteem)
Has anything I've said or done
Ever been of help to anyone.

Has there ever been a spark
Is there anywhere I've left my mark,
Or have I through my life-span crept
And all this time remained inept.

Can I re-arrange my mind
And leave the negative behind
Apply myself in different ways
To profit my remaining days.

If by some simply happy chance
Another's life I could enhance
Would I supply the leading light
To set him on a path that's right?

R H Gunston

DEAR MOTHER

Mother dear
  have no fear
    I'm never coming back,
      belonging here
        shed not a tear
          I've had it with your Jack.

I've met a lover
  she's like no other
    we're getting wed tomorrow,
      which is why I write
        on this very night
          I need something to borrow.

So send the dough
  to us down here below
    and I'll love you 'til you die,
      you've all that money
        I'm not being funny
          and you know I never lie.

Oh mother dear
  please listen here
    you know I'm gone for good,
      but I remember this
        through childhood bliss
          we'll always be flesh and blood.

Ernest Petts

EULOGY FOR A GRANDFATHER

Do not grieve for our grandfather, recently departed,
for with his loved ones, he is now reunited.
Let not your thoughts linger over his death,
for like the falling of an autumn leaf,
so in time will pass your grief.
Think of the good times we have spent together,
you, I and my grandfather.
Remember him as he was, loyal, true and steadfast,
a man proud to the very last.
Remember him at a time when he was happy and let
not a tear form within your eye,
picture him at someone's party, wearing his favourite
frilly shirt and bow tie.
Think not of him as being dead but rather of the
long and good life he lived instead.
We have all spent many happy hours as part of his
family, so for the passing of Albert, do not you weep,
for many pleasant memories of him, have we, in our
hearts to keep.
So until some day we do meet again with him,
along some heavenly dell,
we must say goodnight grandfather, we bid you well.

Phillip N Dawson

VICIOUS CIRCLE

Birth was distressing - roused from her dreams,
She was thrust from the womb shrieking terrified screams,
Ripped from her lifeline, both bruised and distraught,
She was rudely deprived of the comfort she sought.

She married a man that she met on a train,
Five years of happiness, twenty of pain,
She cried when he left, till the tears fell no more,
And she struggled alone with the daughter she bore.

Death took her slowly, through gradual disease,
Though the drugs were a breakthrough the pain wouldn't ease,
And the nurses force-fed her - she couldn't resist,
Till slumped in a wheelchair, she ceased to exist.

Her daughter gave birth in the following year,
To a small wrinkled baby that cried out in fear,
In the arms of her mother she first heard her name,
And the circle of life carried on just the same.

Vivienne Mulhall

HINDSIGHT

Suddenly, it seems the children have grown,
They wish to leave the palatial home,
Life on their own, they think it is fine,
They're departing from me, when I thought they were mine.

The house is so sad, so strange, so quiet,
It seems to have died, I'm alone at night,
The silence is shouting out; how will I cope,
My whole world has changed, I just sit and mope.

Realisation sets in; we all do the same,
Not knowing that we are causing real pain,
Parents who've loved and adored them for years,
End up wondering why? And shed more real tears.

New families begin, new babies are born,
Parents come round, from feeling forlorn,
As nannies etc; they find there's new hope,
When the house is more noisy, and with babies to *cope,*

Life is now again very grand, the house rings out anew,
Grandchildren galore, they're all the same brew,
The days are now full, more than ever before,
Sadness is an old memory, and I'm loving what's in store.

Phyllis Wright

LIFE OF THE CIRCLES

The circle of life has been broken by me:
Unchristened, unmarried - I'm thankfully free!

I'll not father children to worries and pain
to wars of we humans for power or gain -
all-grasping, all-grabbing of things we don't need.
Destruction of nature - this mainly for greed!
The worship of money and sex: misnamed love;
all man-made religions that squabble and shove -
their servants' hypocrisy, failings and cant;
while governments selfishly argue and rant.
The rabbiting parents with lessening space:
unplanning, uncaring - their kids a disgrace!
We've indolence, poverty, dealing in drugs;
possessions and envy; the mugging by thugs,
gang-bangings and murders - far worsening crime.
All hurry and scurry: addiction to time.
Incompetence, avarice, coveted things;
gross gambling and betting with heartache this brings.
Much drunkenness, thoughtlessness, fecklessness, hate,
more tortures and cruelties. And hideous fate:
For all population - growth surely will cause
worse famines, diseases, mass-slaughters and wars.
Our goodness is faded and swamped by the bad
in a world growing rapidly soulless and mad.

Till death, I shall curse this sad turmoil and strife,
then joyfully leave human circles of life.

Tony Hughes-Southwart

FAMILY TREE

In my lovely family tree
we have sown
four generations.
Starting from the top branch
and working my way slowly down,
there is great grandmother
and we all love her,
she is always there
to lend a listening ear.
Times change so she does not interfere.
Then there is me, the grandmother,
a lovely woman,
and there is no other
to compare,
besides who would dare.
I am unique. Next the mother,
my daughter,
who some say is a beautiful granddaughter.
She is helpful and happy, because I taught her.
The recent arrival is a gorgeous baby boy,
the great grandson
who's spoilt rotten.
You wonder why,
the answer is clear.
He's a lovely little dear,
and he's the first male
in our family tree.

Rosemary Medland

OLD

All wrapped up sat here in my chair,
With hearing aid, glasses and a mop
of grey hair.
Thinking of life as it is today,
Thinking of how it was yesterday.
Yesterday in my youth
When life was so full.
Now like the weather
Life is grey and dull.
Oh where did the years go
The years of my life.
When I was somebody's mother,
Somebody's wife.
When you grow old, why do they
not care,
To find love and comfort
Is something quite rare.
So please I say to you
remember,
Sooner than you think,
May will turn to September.

Christine Hall

DEATH IS NEVER FOR EVER

Do not grieve nor mourn at my passing,
I will never be too far away,
Shed no tears of sadness tomorrow,
Rather smile for our yesterday.

In your memories remember the good times,
For the bad times were only mistakes,
We all learned from when we were together,
The kind that everyone makes.

Rejoice for our time spent together,
Don't be sad when you mention my name,
For death is never for ever,
And I know we will all meet again.

James C Watt

LETTING GO

We only had a few years together.
You taught me so much,
I could not believe how happy we were,
I knew I had to make a sacrifice,
For loving you so much.
I did not realise the total price
When you left this earth.
I felt such agony and pain,
I felt I had been torn apart,
I could not go through that suffering again.
My life it was in ruins,
My hopes turned into ashes,
I felt helplessness,
Because you were not there.
My anger was so terrible,
I would never love again,
No-one cared or understood,
I did not want to go on living,
Why couldn't it just end.
It was not my time to leave this earth.
You pick up the pieces,
Then try and let go,
Letting go is the hardest part.
It is not an easy thing to face,
Getting back into the human race.

Doreen Fraser

WHO AM I?

When I was born, I was somebody's daughter,
When I was married, I was somebody's wife,
When I had children, I was somebody's mother,
When I was needed, I was somebody's friend,
When I was working, I was a pillar of society,
When I was disabled, I was somebody's problem,
When I am dead, I'll belong to me.

Linda Storer Smith

A DREAMER

I'm a lonely person sometimes
My thoughts go very deep
Everything going round my head
Especially when I'm asleep.

I've dreamt of distant places
Or places I have been
And remember all the pleasure
That little things can bring.

The times I've walked the cliff paths
On cold and wintry days
The sea so wild and angry
That makes you feel ablaze.

Also remember the good times
On sunny afternoons
Then things can be so special
Forgetting all the glooms.

The years go by so quickly
We all grow up so fast
But then it's nice
Remembering the past.

Patricia Jean Cocking

BITTERSWEET SIXTEEN

I don't think that this teenage thing's all it's cracked up to be.
I'm at the *in-between* age and it's not much fun for me.
Nobody understands me and no-one seems to care.
Too young to go out drinking; too old to pay half fare.

Mom says 'Why don't you act your age?' and that just makes me wild.
She ought to see how all the teachers treat me like a child.
'You're old enough to marry.' I have often heard them quote,
And though that sounds all well and good, I'm still too young to vote.

My older friends are working and I really can't defend
The way I'm green with envy when I see how much they spend.
But I can't see that working hard is any use to me,
I'd have to work my socks off just to pass GCSE.

I'm sure that being this age is the worst of all by far;
Too old for playing children's games, too young to drive a car.
I've often heard that teenage years are filled with utter bliss,
But, frankly, I'd be quite content to give it all a miss.

These silly regulations and all these laws and rules
Are thought up by MPs and other geriatric fools.
I only wish that I could get my own back on the lot.
I'd pass a law that people over fifty should be shot.

No-one ever listens, they just tell me what to do.
They don't seem to think that I could have a point of view.
They say I must be patient but that drives me up the wall:
I can't wait for years and years; it's *now* I know it all!

Dennis Turner

NO USE TO THEM ANYMORE

They tell me
I am no use to them anymore,
That I have completed my obligations,
And a new man has arrived to fill my shoes.

And so I walk away
With thirty years and a gold watch,
Not much consolation,
For a lifetime's devotion,
I thought I had more to offer,
But it seems progression
Has finally caught up with me.
And abandoned me
To a life
On the old aged pension scrap heap.

They tell me everything has to change,
And I agreed,
But what makes me sad is the way people
change towards me.
When I am no use to them anymore.

Andrew Collins

KEEP A BRAVE HEART

Precarious as life may seem
When youth instils the heart with dreams
The game of chance soon won or lost
A wealth of time to count the cost.

Relentlessly though much maligned
The labour of Old Father Time
Remoulds us gently without pain
Unnoticed as we strive to gain.

Reflecting in the latter years
Through misty eyes awash with tears
On deviations in life's course
How well we understand remorse.

But when the thread of life is worn
From this existence we are torn
Fear not eternity alone
For life is just a stepping stone . . .

Lynda M Bourne

GROWING UP

Once it was nappies,
And bottles galore,
Baby walkers,
And toys on the floor,
Noisy rattles, and musical chimes
Lullabies and nursery rhymes.

Now it's boots and a mini skirt,
Wearing make-up, and being a flirt,
Taking notice of all the boys,
Playing CDs - what a noise,
For disco nights,
- Black tights,
- Shoulders bare,
And curled hair.

Oh they've grown up so fast,
The years have flown past,
From babes in arms,
To teenagers, full of girlie charms,
I just hope they'll be happy,
Whatever they do,
And then, as their mother,
I'll be happy too.

Karen E Poad

ROLL BACK THE YEARS

Roll back the years
That I may see once more
My happy children
Playing on the shore.

What happy days
But oh, how quickly passed
How sad such precious moments
Do not last.

Let me recall
The best days of my life,
Those years spent as a mother
And a wife.

Draw back the curtains
Let me see your face
And let me feel again
Your warm embrace.

The years roll by
Like chapters of a book.
Should we not pause
And take a backward look?

Then in our hearts
Remember with a smile
Those little things which made
Our life worthwhile.

Anne Bonsen

STARTING OVER . . . AGAIN!

Memories of passion, heartache and strain
Endless love and endless pain

Got to learn to live again
Got to sing a sweet refrain

New beginning, brand new start
Found my love, lost my heart
End of heartache, passions aflame
New songs to sing, I'm living again . . .

Lying in your arms
Bewitched by your charms
Lying in your arms
Again

I stare into your eyes
Completely mesmerised
I stare into your eyes
Again

Harping on the past
Wondering when at last
Her loving eyes won't haunt me any more

Lying in your arms
Devoted to *her* charms
I'm lying in my head
Again . . .

S Friede

EVERY DAY

Every day we should have a Funday,
Put a smile on our face.
Every day, yes even a Monday,
Give humour its place.
Every day we should be happy.
Every day let's not be blue.
But I know that there can be sad times in life,
and it's true.
That's life it's true!

Every day I walk down the old road,
That Memory Lane.
Every day I'm not feeling too cold,
Those warm times remain.
Every day you can be happy.
Lighten up those shades of blue.
But I know that there can be sad times in life,
and it's true.
That's life it's true!

Every day it writes me a record,
A page for my book.
Every day I'm keeping a record,
For each day when I look.
Every day you can be happy.
In-between those shades of blue.
But I know that there can be sad times in life,
and it's true.
That's life it's true!

Graham Mitchell

REMEMBERING BRUCE

Once we had a dog named Bruce
We reared him from a pup.
Later we had children
Together they grew up.
But time passed by the kids grew up
Bruce no longer was a pup.
He found it hard to struggle on
To greet us at the door,
Then one day I'm sad to say
Bruce, he was no more.
We wept for him, we missed him so
Our faithful pal so true,
If there's a heaven for dogs I know
There'll be a place for you.
Now we have another pup.
She really is quite sweet
I'm sure if you were still around
You would get on a treat.
She fills the gap you left behind
A lovely little lass
We thought of lots of names for her
And then we called her Cass
Sometimes when I look at her
I see you standing there
For in our hearts
You'll always be
A memory to share.

Kerrie Derbyshire

A TIME FOR EVERYTHING

There is a time for everything
Underneath the sun
A time to be born
And a time to die
That's how it is for everyone
But what happens to us in-between
The cradle and the tomb
We live a life
The best we can
From the moment we leave
       the womb.
We may be rich
We may be poor
Plain or fair of face
Very special or just ordinary
Each one of us has our place
We love we hate
We laugh and cry
Feel pain and pleasure too
Happy and sad
Young and old
Wonderfully made it's true.

Christine Williams

YEW TREE

We found a seedling yew-tree
In a child's garden bed,
Two inches high - 'A little fern'
The budding gardener said,

And planted it with her toy spade
Firm in the orchard grass;
A ring of pebbles kept the place
From wandering feet that pass.

No fern, her yew outstrips the house
With a half-century's height
And this, the childhood of a tree,
Passed like a summer night

To bole and leaf and coral fruit;
But now the little maid
Has wings of grey in her dark hair,
And acts severe and staid.

Bevil Grenville

IT'S MY LIFE

As I flip through my 'book of life',
I view the passing years,
There I see joy and laughter,
Some anxiety and tears.

As a small child - time passed slow,
Oh - how I longed to be grown up,
To do exactly as I wished -
To take my own 'pot luck'.

But children do not realise -
The hard work that's involved -
To achieve all you want from life,
To get all your problems solved.

Employment, marriage, children,
These things all take their toll,
But - oh the fun, I did enjoy,
'Til I realised my goal.

Well, now that I've retired,
The years pass by so fast,
I'm cramming in - all I can each day -
And will do - 'til the last.

D M Jennings

THREE SCORE YEARS AND TEN

Life starts simple, eat, drink, cry, sleep
an easy start but hard to keep
Then through the passage of childhood years
when growing up amongst your peers
who really seem so important then
we model ourselves to be like them.
Along then comes sweet adolescence
the joy and pain of sexual experiments.
Clumsy fumblings, 'til we get it right
or worse we get it wrong.
A home, a car, a family
Big decisions now, not one but three
lives linked together.
Then the worries about the job, the bills, the kids
until they grow up and leave you with
yourselves again
Fear of dying comes as both get older
joints get stiffer, winters colder.
Suddenly the two are one
not really one, but half of one
that lived a life together.
Now just waiting for the day
the pain and loneliness goes away
and a life which started with such zest
will flick a switch and turn to death.

Michael Turley

CIRCLES

Twisting, turning, crossing, weaving,
Lacing, flowing, threading, inter-locking,
Celtic Circles.

Beginning, playing, growing, learning,
Maturing, searching, ageing, ending,
Life's Circles.

Iris E Limb

THE CIRCLE OF LIFE

In sweet Oslo, lies Vigliand park,
Where the mason's chisel left its mark,
Breath-taking scenes of man and wife,
From birth to death, from the circle of life.

Poignant scene of babe-in-arms,
Life-like form with many charms
Later still with consternation,
Stamping his foot in indignation.

Another stage of life is past.
To his new love he holds fast,
Wedding bells ring out with joy,
The union's blessed with a baby boy.

He in turn, like father's life,
Takes unto himself a wife.
As the pattern of life goes on,
This time, it's a daughter and son.

The boy who stamped his foot at life,
Succumbs to rigours of toil and strife.
Grandparent now but frail and old,
The story end, he leaves untold.

There is no end as life goes on
And offspring has a baby son,
Who takes unto himself a wife;
He must not break the circle of life.

Rita O'Rourke

JOAN

I tried to write a poem
about the one I love
The sparkle in her eyes would be
like all the stars above

I would tell about the golden rays
of sunlight in her hair
But I remembered arguments
and heartache and despair

When love we had was tossed aside
and tempers ruled our heads
And cruel words we didn't mean
were better left unsaid

But following the darkest sky
the sun again will shine
And heartache almost seems worthwhile
when our arms once more entwine

Love cannot be taken
from selected lines of prose
It is sometimes like the nettle
not always like the rose

My feelings are not measured
by rhyme or sweet refrain
It is only by the joy I feel
when she is mine again

David Guy Prosser

VAIN REGRETS

I often sit in vain regret
Thinking of years that were ill-spent
If I could turn my foot-steps back
I'd work hard to amend my tracks.

Black shadows loom before my eyes
With memories that refuse to die
Reminders of my ill-spent years
Close in in deep regret and tears.

Why to blind folly did I go
Nor stop to think what went before
I did not learn from my mistakes
Till outcome proved I still had strayed.

I would not listen to advice
Though others tried to clear my sight
Resentment rose within my chest
When all they wanted was to help.

Why did I sit and stare in school
When lessons were taught in the room
Correction failed to make me stop
To renew my mind and to take stock.

If I could now renew the past
I'd take the road back to success
I'd word hard to redeem the times
And prove that I could turn the tide.

I swear I would work hard at school
And prove to all I'm not a fool
I'd make a name to make me proud
And make up for wasted hours.

Katie S Macdonald

THE WHEEL TURNS FULL CIRCLE

Impatiently we tolerate our elders,
They always seem to be ahead of us.
When we are born we are helpless,
We are at their mercy,
They feed and clothe us,
They come in the night when we cry,
Comfort and reassure us, give us
Our favourite teddy.
When we reach a certain age,
We don't need them, they seem to
Think we still need them.
We always seem to be in the wrong,
They know everything, never wrong,
We never know what they think,
They always seem to know what we think.
When we marry and have children
Of our own, then we understand.
We run to them for advice, as
Our children will run to us
For advice. The wheel turns full circle.

Gerry Kenny

THE ROAD OF TIME

We all must make the journey
Along the road of time
And simple pleasures once enjoyed
Seem left so far behind
As unwittingly surrender we
Unto life's dreary grind

The sudden understanding
That life must move along
And we are just the singers
Not the writers of its song.

For time she takes us on
And bends us to her will
When all we ask is yesterday
Today's a bitter pill.

George Newton

THE PURPOSE

Onward, onward ever forward
Through life's cycle on we go,
Always searching, never finding
The answer to our being so.

Here to rule or tread lightly
Treat our fellow well or not,
Who's to say which path to follow;
What the purpose, is this our lot?

Born to follow this convention,
Live our life as others say.
Work to eat, to multiply,
Continue in life's one long play.

Comedy or tragedy,
Does it really matter which?
If there really is a reason
Someone show me where's my niche?

Now I've found it without trying,
I feel peaceful as a dove;
Days too short, cannot stop smiling
Why is this? I've fallen in love.

Pamela E Potter

GONE - NOT FORGOTTEN
(To Shane)

I never really thought you'd ever leave me,
It seemed as though you were invincible,
but I was wrong - today you died.

I was in a haze of tears - I still am,
as the last breaths left your body, I stoked your head -
I didn't want you to die - but I couldn't stop you.

You looked so frightened in your paralysed state,
and I was frightened for you, but all I could do was
caress you, and whisper how much I loved you.

I have never felt so helpless before now,
When I watched you loosen and slip away,
I held on - praying that you would awaken -
but you couldn't.

You were taken at almost 5 o'clock before even
Spring had arrived,
You never got to see the sun of Summer '96
nor even feel the April rain.

Now my world is different - the most important love
is gone,
I am left with a cold body - where the life and
soul have evaporated, but yet,

You were so old, as I am often reminded - but to me,
You seemed so young.
You have left me though with so many happy memories,
which I will always cherish.

Shane - I wish you hadn't left,
but I am thankful that I was there for you when you
were dying -
and even though I feel empty and lost -
I will follow you - wait for me?

Olivia Kennedy

THE CIRCLE OF LIFE

Looking back -
Was it only yesterday I was in the spring of my life?
Entering into - the circle of life;
Like a bud begging to be a leaf on a tree,
That blossoms for bees,
And flowers into seeds.

All too soon -
Discarding dolls, thinking I was too old,
Rushing into - the circle of life;
Like many a-child, reaching pastures new,
I took in the view,
And into a teenager grew.

Then blooming -
With offspring, my darling seedlings of life;
The dolls - they came to life;
Now children from the buds of May.
And as their Mother, I did discover,
They'd become my summer.

Looking back -
Entering into the Autumn of my life;
As leaves become golden on the family tree -
The tree of life;
With grandchildren, I discover,
Memories are much fonder.

Looking back -
The child in the circle of life;
Gathering winter woollies and a cosy shawl;
Wishing I could stay -
All I can say -
Is - was it only yesterday?

G Bedford

THE CHRISTENING

The baby being sick for the third time heralded the Christening day
Mother frantically wiping the effects from her once pristine
dress, anxiously awaits relatives on their way.
Dad, uncomfortable in unaccustomed tie, struggles to hide from
this insanity
Wishing already the day was over, and life might return to its
mundane normality.
At last ushered to the church the group assembles with unease,
Surrounded by the trappings of a little known God, who through
the reciting of their vows they seek to appease.
The baby yells, the priest's monotone rises to drown this shrill
small voice,
Holy admittance gained, the deed is done, flashlights pop and
out they go, relieved and released at last to rejoice.
Looking forward to the tea, sandwiches, wine and cake,
Forgetting in an instant, the vicar, the church and the promises
that a short while before they had been required to make.
And so the child was named amid this frantic whirl,
Sensing her debut was over, her role sufficiently played,
She slept, this tired little girl.

Mary Spence

FULL CIRCLE

As a baby I depended on mother
To look after me and my big brother.
Starting school didn't seem so bad
With all the loving care we'd had.

Teenage years, exams to pass.
A desire to be top of the class.
Late teens, no-one could tell me then,
'You must be home by half-past ten.'

University years went by so fast,
Now seem like a mirage in the past.
Looking for the perfect job,
Trying to beat the rest of the mob.

A few years later, marriage came.
A change in home and job and name.
And soon a new life will begin.
I think that this is where I came in!

Angela Ballester

DUCKLING'S DEBUT

I watched you glide across the pond
Your little ducklings formed a bond
All about was bright and new
As one by one they followed you.

You circled about they followed suite
Undisturbed by frog or newt
Their little legs as paddles used
Kept me happy and amused.

You headed for the grass so green
To have a rest and have a preen
Up the bank the ducklings scrambled
One didn't care and he just ambled
Another slipped into the pond
Only then did you respond.

Fluffy down all soft and clean
Their little bodies thin and lean
A month or two and they'll outgrow
The Mother who they used to know
And on that pond, the very same
The duck and ducklings will remain.

Frances Bennell

PLAYFUL SHADOWS

When the day gives way to a moonlit night
And long shadows creep down the vale,
And a gentle breeze blows through the trees,
Creating a high pitched wail.

The old trees murmur and rustle their leaves
To the breeze blowing gently through,
As it makes the young trees sway with ease,
In a game that they once knew.

As the moon's cold light strikes each swaying tree,
A dark shadow grows out from its base
Covering the ground, arms waving around,
But hid from the moon's beaming face.

The shadows all know the moon's beaming face
Can't see them, wherever they go,
Yet, out of sight, they depend on his light
Whilst the breeze blows the trees to and fro.

The moon climbs up higher in the night sky.
Then the breeze blows some white clouds past.
They hide the moon, the breeze plays its tune.
Trees sway, but no shadows are cast.

Then dawn breaks out and fresh shadows appear.
The moon fades, he's not at his best.
As the sun's warm light rolls back the night,
The moon sinks away in the west.

The sun's warm light makes the new shadows strong
As the trees are caught by its rays.
They wait for the breeze to blow through the trees,
So the night's game then becomes day's.

John B Briggs

BRAHMSIAN

Through walls of water
It steps,
Defiantly dry,
Hard along jagged stepping stones
Left over from giants' play.
It leaps and skips, kicking
Little skipping stones in front,
Until it plunges suddenly
Up, along marble,
Water streaming down,
And announces: 'Stop! Here I Am.'

Alice Colby

THE LEAVING

We were leaving this house after thirteen very happy and very sad years,
A house of love laughter and bitter acrid tears,
Buying it with what seemed like a hefty mortgage, that had descended,
By luck and good fortune, four years after the war had ended,
Another eight years and it could have been ours, no sweat no fuss,
But we'd seen this brand new one and decided that was for us,
It was detached instead of semi, yet in spite of this there were many,
Things that we would miss, strange that it had taken this,
To bring memories back and find, that they lived so clearly in the mind,
Happiness and sadness raw had rested 'neath this roof,
Welding us closer together as if in proof,
Of what God joins together, let no man tear asunder,
He paused within the empty hall, and felt that he could hear it call,
Goodbye farewell and good luck to you all,
Then he was outside and pulling the front door closed,
Climbing into the car he seemed to hear a voice,
Ringing in his head saying, don't worry you've made the right choice.

R H Higgins

FAMILY ALBUM

The first cry, a breath of air,
Chuckles and smiles, a wisp of hair.
Cameras clicking, flashlights bright,
All we need is a restful night!
Crawling, shuffling, toddling along,
Running and tumbling, 'My knee hurts Mum!'
School days, best days, if only they knew,
Exams are looming, so much to get through.
First day at college, it takes a while
To find new friends, start a new lifestyle.
The wedding's set for June, it seems
Our daughter's to wed the man of her dreams.
Time has flown by; memories so dear,
Photographs to cherish each precious year.
An album so full of life's joy and fears,
The sun goes down and our eyes fill with tears.

Avril Reay

YOU SMILED UP

No numerous eyes
around your sidelines
waiting in painful
anticipation.
        You chose
        your time
        your final departing.
Held your hand
Stroked your brow
You smiled up
at my I love you.
Then like a flick of a switch
        you left me.

Diane C Shanks

IMMORTAL EYES

Flesh is but a substance, as
is skin and bone,
We sign out at the start of
life, like signing for a loan.
Our teeth although enamel and
cared for night and day,
They give way in the passing
years, to that old thief decay.
Now hair we have to harvest,
when the time is right,
But as the years recede by,
the harvest becomes light.
But eyes, they are immortal,
their recycled when it's time,
Perhaps my great grandchildren,
one day shall see through mine.

Rodney Emanuel Lipman

I'M A MUM

Today it was fun for me and my son
It's not every day he makes me feel like a mum
I felt wanted, loved and needed too
And when I looked up the skies they were blue
I was washing, cleaning and still found time to spare
For the games you play with your child here and there
A spin in the car - it was a treat
To see him smile as he passed me a sweet
Tomorrow will be different I know
But today I'm with him and I feel a glow
I'm his friend and he's my chum
I feel happy inside just being mum

Carol Crean

THE BIRTH

Red kiss marks covered Jane's cheeks
when Paul gave out on his emotions.
He forcefully plastered kisses galore, as never before.
I am here, I am here darling, don't worry, I am here!

She knows you're here, that is for sure!
You would have been better off pacing to and fro!
Behind that closed and locked door!
The nurse snapped in disgust, give her a break!

Beads of sweat covered Jane's brow as she moaned and groaned
in between breaks of trying to deliver the baby.
They said it would be hard, her first and last.
She was exhausted and low as she groaned.

Eventually a baby boy entered our world, Jane sighed, at last!
The nurse took hold of him, her face full of grief.
She started to smack his bottom, again and again,
Come on yell, for hell's sake yell! She shouted in distress,
Gave him the kiss of life, again and again, then oxygen.

The other nurse mopped and stroked Jane's brow to comfort
She asked she a blue baby, is he dying? No was the answer,
he is a lovely pink baby boy, she said in disbelief, so aware.

She knew they were struggling between life and death, waiting,
for miracles, a cat in hell's chance, accoutrement attending.
Take the oxygen away, he used all his skills on the baby.
Suddenly the baby squealed, let out a big cry.
Was granted the cat's chance, it was worth that try.

Thank God, thank God! Jane cried with sigh and quivering lips.
With tears streaming down her face as Paul kissed her lips.
Kept on kissing, saying he's alive, he's alive!
Like a mad man he shouted over and over, he didn't die, didn't die!
Then he must have been sent was the reply!

Vera Radcliffe

WIDOWHOOD

So now you are a woman, alone
and you need to be understood.
Well, I know how you feel
So I'll help you along my way;
      through widowhood.

My answer, to grief, is simple;
I'll share it with you - if I may?
So, widows of the world, unite!
Let's fight, for a happier day!

Help others! That's my secret!
Live on - do things the same!
Give God a go: who blessed the
day; you took your loved one's name.

I know how much, you miss him!
Those arms, which held you tight!
Like me; you're alone, through the
wee - small hours: no husband in the night.

Start each day, with a gallant smile!
Don't grieve, for what might have been!
For there is no perfect marriage
there's not one, that I have seen.

Smile, at the little fights you had
and how things turned out right.
Then blush, at the way, you made up!
Until the morning light!

Believe that he can see you
make him proud of you, through the years.
Then one day; he'll kiss the face he loved
When you leave, this vale of tears.

Patricia Mary-Gross

213

WHEN THE LAST OFFSPRING LEAVES HOME

When the last offspring leaves home,
The impact is strong,
The home is so empty,
Will the days be so long?

We'll get used to the changes,
But time it will take,
Many people go through this,
For goodness sake!

Our home is so tidy now,
It's the first time for years,
And we can open the phone bill,
No horror or fear.

There's room in the wash-basket,
No clothes on the floor,
The top's on the toothpaste,
It never was before.

No nagging and shouting,
'The soggy bath-towel's on the bed'
No,'Can't tidy today mum,
Tomorrow instead.'

But tomorrow never did come,
It all stayed the same,
The kids were so untidy,
Were we to blame?

So you see there's a plus side,
And when all's said and done,
It's not easy bringing kids up,
Whether daughter or son.

Linda M Porter

A POEM FOR EARTH

The pollution which we're creating, is killing all the trees,
But it seems we have no time, to care for things like these.

The Earth is important to live out our days, but there will be no life, unless we change our ways.

The animals are dying, we have to help them now, from everything like giraffe and elephant, to tiger and cow.

The changes are coming, but no-one hardly knows, until everything we care for, just vanishes and goes.

We should bring to our attention the rainforests and their task, because we are abusing them they're not going to last.

The trees, they give us oxygen, and shield us from the weather, Mother Nature is telling us we could change things forever.

Mother Earth is crying and calling to us now, so for future generations, we have to teach them how.

Danielle Bevens (12)

DONNY

My precious little friend,
You meant the world to me,
You will live forever in my heart,
And in my memory,
You were so very special
From the day that you were born,
Like the very special sunrise,
Or the lark at early dawn,
Your very special presence,
Upon this earth with me,
My darling little pet.
No more your face I'll see.

Elizabeth Walker

215

THE WEDDING

Hairdresser comes at half past eight.
Bride's Mother gets into a state.
The Father waits and sheds a tear,
for his daughter to appear.
He paces the room, left and right,
then sees his girl all dressed in white.
She looks so pretty, so petite.
Looks so happy, smells so sweet.
The horse and carriage wait outside,
for the Father and the Bride.
At last they come out onto the street.
The neighbours cheer, oh what a treat.
In the carriage the Bride does sit.
The time is getting on a bit.
At the church the Groom does wait,
for his Bride, who is late.
The Wedding March begins to play.
Everyone stands and looks away.
Towards the Father and the Bride,
who walk together side by side.
Down the Aisle, to her man,
who will take her by the hand.
Exchange vows and wedding rings.
The organ plays. The Choir sings.
Now they are Husband and Wife.
They hope to have a happy life.
Outside, everyone must pose,
when the Camera man takes photos.
Everything's a great success.
Lots of joy and happiness.

Sharon Lydia Rowe

THE FINAL CUL-DE-SAC

Life collaborates with memories
Hiring portions of our youth
To view at our convenience as the middle age hormones brew
Life bribes us with concessions
Selling diverse contraband
And barricades the road to retirement with elderly juvenile clans

Age splutters with inconsistency
Excepting manners from the wild
As behavioural patterns alternate 'tween high snobbery and a child
The mind excels in ignorance trying on umpteen paper masks
Then running down the side street into a silent cul-de-sac

Rebellious minds all congregate asking comfort to ease their plight
Pleading for personal time walks to escape the circle of life
Some steal the eternal elixir hiding birthdays in its lair
Hoping the days they confiscate will fit the age they wear

They quarrel with the inventory
Of rules that life has wrote
That condemn the over fifties to the far edges of the moat
The lambs conspire with nature
To kidnap the mutton mask
And ransom out the moment for a walk into the past

Life becomes a short term mutiny
Murdering vogue for disco themes
With middle aged feme coverts all dressed has dancing queens
Seen has traitors of society scattering treason on the floor
Gathering one last act of anarchy before the closing of the door

The rebellion shrivels with embarrassment into reflections in a pool
With a statement of self-judgement to exonerate the fool
The guilty settle for probation and the last sacrificial pact
As the road straightens to retirement and the final cul-de-sac

David Bridgewater

WITH THIS RING

'With this ring, I thee wed'
These words you vowed to me
And promised me a love to last
Throughout life's stormy seas

You were all I ever wanted
And I was proud your wife to be
A gentle heart, a tower of strength
And you loved only me

Our union brought children
Our happiness was complete
My cup was full, I was content
And life was very sweet

But somehow, somewhere I lost you
I did not see the signs
Another stole your love away
And broke this heart of mine

You took my love and crushed it
You broke my faith and trust
My anchor's gone and I'm adrift
And leave you now I must

'Till death us do part'
Do you recall
These words you vowed to me?
I remember and with my dying breath
I now set you free

Glenda Greeson

DOORNAILS

Dead as a doornail?

So what do doornails know
Of being dead?
Like rocks
And rounded stones
And pebbles on the beach,
They've neither dread
Nor comprehension
Of being dead
Nor apprehension
Of what is still to come:
No tension
Mars their day,
They never say
Enough!
But merely continue to be
All unaware
Of you and me,
Of grief and laughter
And all hereafter,
The now, and forever . . .
. . . And ever.

Hal Cheetham

FOR US, FOR THEM, FOR YOU, FOR ME

There are no phone lines to heaven -
No brass polished letterbox there,
When mothers are called home to heaven -
We must wait to visit them there.

A florist can never deliver -
And lunch overlooking a river,
With moments to share, with moments to care -
Are lost in the mists of sometime and somewhere.

Her caress for a falling down, fallen down leg-
A kiss for an 'I've bumped me 'ead,'
A mender of clothes, a mender of those -
With broken hearts when love departs.

That path to her door with its welcoming gate
No need to knock nor hesitate,
When wicked we'd be, sometimes wicked we were
She's scold for a moment with eyes that adored.

She who'd not your secrets tell
Who hid her disappointments well,
She who by your shoulder stood
When no-one would although they could.

A mother like no other for no other could there be,
And when her time is over here-in lies tragedy.
A love beyond compare for we most surely see,
There is no love like a mother's love -
For us, for them, for you, for me.

Philip Joseph Mee

RICHES

Give me words for jewels
To polish and refine,
And I will string a necklace
All others to outshine,
To fling around the universe
This glittering wealth of mine.

Pearls of dew-drop beauty
Nurtured out of sight
In underwater stillness
Brought from dark to light,
Glowing with a radiance soft
Enhancing, tear-drop bright.

Garland green of emerald
A girdle round the world,
Of velvet moss and springing grass
And budding leaf upcurled,
The ever-living robe of earth
In fragrant foliage furled.

Deep-dyed red of rubies
Crimson drops of life,
Bleeding heart of wounded love
Pierced as with a knife,
Flowing stream of human blood
Spilling out in strife.

So - give me words for riches
Vocal gems to twine,
Un-fading in the jewel box
In settings to enshrine,
The precious stones of meaning
Within this wealth of mine.

Joan Baker

BE POSITIVE

Be positive, don't give in,
With determined thought you are sure to win.

The summit you aim for need not be high,
With positive thought you can reach for the sky.

Some days you feel weary and terribly sad,
You look back on memories when times weren't so bad.

But with positive thought the sun will shine through,
And there is no limit to the things you can do.

Try not to be sad and let things get you down,
Wear a smile in place of a frown.

Love, laugh and be happy everyday,
For nothing can take those feelings away.

Stand firm to your goal, don't be swayed,
And in time the darkness will begin to fade.

So say to yourself 'It's time to live,'
Be happy . . . Be joyful . . .
Be Positive!

Sarah Anne

REFLECTIONS

Grandfather clock ticks on in the hall
It hasn't seemed that long at all
Since we were wed, and young at heart
Made our vows we'd never part.

Along came babies, life was sweet,
So soon the patter of tiny feet
Growing strong with love and care
Hands were full, no time to spare.

School days were a time of pleasure
Making gifts for us to treasure,
Joyful moments, sometimes sad,
Keeping up with the latest fad.

Through the teenage years they past
Boy meets girl, the bond was cast
Love that blossomed, it's the circle of life
Brought together as man and wife.

With grandchildren we soon were blessed
No moments of peace, no time to rest,
Repeating the scene just as before
When our own little ones were the age of four.

Now with memories fading, eyes getting dim
He looks at me, I look at him
As side by side we sit and recall
While grandfather clock still ticks in the hall.

Janice Richer

26.22 MILES
*(For no 20516 'Sparky' who ran for
the Cancer Relief Macmillan Fund)*

L ithe and lean,
O bligated, keen.
N imble to aspire
D o sponsors desire.
O nward we cry,
N ever say die.

M arathon man
A utomaton
R acing by
A nno Domini.
T ime is paced,
H arrier in haste,
O ne objective
N ow subjective.
　　　　　in
9　　　　ninety
5　　　　five.

Jennifer Wright

CANCER

The cancer that doth grow, up until soon we did not know.
You look at me with lonesome eyes,
As I listen to your uneven breaths and sighs.
I see the pain travel right through your body, you are unaware I was once
your best buddy.
Sucking through a straw your nutritional drink as you have not the strength
to eat.

You would have shivered even in extreme heat.
You look so weak, you look so sad how could someone as great and supportive
of everyone could have changed so much in such a short time.
Your life is just pain, you must be envious of mine.
Never a smile always a tear, but we both do fear as your end drawn near.

Slowly, slowly your time draws near.

Diana Sorrell (13)

THE SONG IN MY HEART

There's a song in my heart the world cannot hear,
For the world would not understand;
The music plays on and on my love,
Though the words of the song were not planned.

Though 'happy endings' may not be,
The music will live on for me
And if some day we have to part
Keep me still within your heart.

If I leave this world before you
Or another love you find,
I know you'll hear the music,
Though the words be left behind.

It may be there's a rainbow
At the journey's end
Where we will meet again some day,
My dear 'Forever Friend'.

And though I dream it may be so,
If dreams are not to be,
Keep the music in your heart . . .
And sometimes think of me.

Margaret Amelia Hall

RE-PARENTHOOD

Babies
Teenagers
Growing up to sixth form.
University
Going up to graduation.
Very proud. Wife's new hat
very loud!
Early marriage
Children come
Off we go again
Memories re-born
With grandchildren.

Ray Nurse

AGE

The tide fast flowing towards it neap,
The fading light, the crescent moon
In its last quarter, dimly poised
Above this purple lip of earth,
Before it dips beyond,
The bald dome, and the wrinkled face
Inscribed, etched with hieroglyphics
The history of a lifetime,
Who, in the mirror, vaguely sees
The phantom of his youth.
Now he has seen the dawn, the noon,
And early eve, and in the dusk
When shrouding mists do fluctuate
Before the coming of the dark
He sees the evening star,
The crowning glory of his life
Is that by death he'll live again
Beyond the rim of night.

J Barnwell

THE PORTRAIT

He turned unto the mirror
Wherein life's portraits dwell,
Looked in vain for the pastel shades
Of youth's bright yet brief spell.
No more now those exquisite lines
That traced his finest days,
Or the deep rich glow like burnished gold
That graced another age.
He saw now but a canvas
Brush-stroked with time's own grey,
Smiled a little sadly,
And from the mirror turned away.

Austin Baines-Brook

GROWING UP

Schooldays are now in times gone by.
The brink of reality; a humble sigh,
I've had my chance to make a hit,
Will my future unfold - bit by bit?
They say schooldays are the best part of life;
About six hours of work, and that's not all strife.
Long holidays stretching out for weeks on end;
Then all of a sudden, you're at life's bend.
Endless days of eight hours at work.
A whole year goes by before holidays lurk.
Those three weeks pass at astonishing speed.
Please, back to school; it's all that I need.
Few responsibilities, no bills to pay.
Now look at the pile that's in my 'in tray'.
There's pressures at work, never safe in the job.
The brink of reality; a humble sigh? No. A sob.

Carol O'Connor

ON BURYING HELEN'S PET RABBIT

Sorrowful young one at my side
watching me bury your pet that died,
sense you the future, perhaps foresee
that much the same will be done with me?

Success or failure, laughter or sorrow
will likely still be ours tomorrow,
and yet this rabbit whose life is spent
stirs a disquieting presentiment.

Shall I lie as calm as he
sinking uncomplainingly
into a place beneath rough lawn
deaf to the calls of every dawn?

Short and restless lives we spend
stacking our follies end on end,
behind the smiling masks of sanity
articulate the bones of vanity.

This animal couldn't philosophise
when sickness came to close his eyes,
without complaint at nature's harshness
his shadow slipped into the darkness.

All life's fragile brief stability
must soon give way to entropy,
so let us only ask to find
acceptance and a quiet mind.

Kenneth Clark

PANDORA'S BOX

A new arrival what a joy,
be it a girl or baby boy.
The apple of a parent's eye,
always there, won't make you cry.

Off to school on the first day,
make new friends then out to play.
Growing up, taking a knock or bump,
now out of an aircraft, you first parachute jump.

Soldier, sailor, doctor or nurse,
always money in wallet or purse.
Love at first sight, a stolen kiss,
Soon to be a Mrs no longer a Miss.

Down the aisle see them walk,
a lovely couple hear people talk.
A mortgage from a society or bank,
your devoted parents you wish to thank.

Off on honeymoon so far away,
sending a postcard every second day.
Alas now aged your parents soon depart,
up to heaven, ah! A broken heart.

Years slowly pass, two happy people,
flick through old photos, see a church and steeple.
Life is but one of nature's clocks,
full of wonder just like Pandora's box.

Dave Wilkie

FUNERAL SONG

There's just a sad wooden cross marking his grave,
A few wild flowers from a nearby field,
No marble, no stone, or pretty poem
The cost of that his family won't yield.

His son stands alone by the vicar's side,
A scattering of friends from times long gone
Before he made his pile, and shut them out
To wallow in wealth, never passing it on.

As mean as Scrooge, this miserly man
Tight-fisted and cold to the end.
His pauper's cross, soon to split and rot
On hallowed ground, is the last he'll spend.

For the man in black is his father's son,
His mother cries by the cross with shock,
Not for him whose heart was long since gone
But for the son, who's from the same old block

There's just a sad wooden cross marking his grave
A few wild flowers from a nearby field.
His son could have built him a Taj Mahal,
But his purse, like his heart, is sealed.

Felicity Howard

FROM TOTS TO TEENS

From one day old to sweet sixteen
And all the ages in between
Our children, either girl or boy
Bring with them problems - and much joy!

Now babies are a great delight
As long as they don't scream all night.
Aren't they supposed to bill and coo,
And not thrown up all over you?

The toddler's always on the go.
And only knows one word - it's *no*
When left alone to play with toys
They choose the one that makes most noise,

When schooldays come there's some relief
A mistaken thought, it's my belief,
It's 'pick me up' or 'run me there'
To cubs or clubs, or perhaps the fair.

You'd think that when they reached their teens
They'd like smart clothes, not ragged jeans.
They're bored with books, TV and dames
They'd rather play computer games.

But all too soon there comes the day
When they decide to go away.
You're left with memories, sweet and sad.
Well after all - kids aren't *all* bad!

Muriel Holland

INFORMATION

We hope you have enjoyed reading this book - and that you will continue to enjoy it in the coming years.

If you like reading and writing poetry drop us a line, or give us a call, and we'll send you a free information pack.

Write to

Arrival Press Information
1-2 Wainman Road
Woodston
Peterborough
PE2 7BU